CHARLES HADDON
SPURGEON
REVISITED

A DRAMATIC BIOGRAPHY

DAVID MALCOLM BENNETT

rhiza press

Charles Haddon Spurgeon Revisited: A Dramatic Biography

Copyright © David Malcolm Bennett 2016
Published by Rhiza Press
www.rhizapress.com.au
PO Box 1519, Capalaba Qld 4157

ISBN: 978-1-925139-69-3

National Library of Australia Cataloguing-in-Publication entry:
Creator: Bennett, David (David Malcolm), 1942- author.
Title: Charles Haddon Spurgeon revisited / David Malcolm Bennett.
ISBN: 9781925139693 (paperback)
Subjects: Spurgeon, C. H. (Charles Haddon), 1834-1892.
Baptists--Great Britain--Clergy--Biography.
Evangelists--Great Britain--Biography.
Preaching--Great Britain.
Dewey Number: 286.142092

CONTENTS

CONTENTS

CHAPTER 1

THE SNOW STORM

When once I mourned a load of sin,
When conscience felt a wound within,
When all my works were thrown away,
When on my knees I knelt to pray,
Then, blissful hour, remembered well,
I learnt Thy love Immanuel! (C H Spurgeon)

No one but a fool would venture out on a day like this. It was extremely cold and the snow fell continuously, covering the fields and footpaths with a pure, white carpet. The savage wind cut through the warmest clothing. But Charles Spurgeon was desperate. It was a Sunday, early in January 1850 and he was trudging through the snow, bracing against the wind. He was looking for a church, a specific church, where he believed that he would hear the word of God, which might set him free from the sin and condemnation that held him bound.

In recent weeks he had visited almost every church in his hometown seeking salvation but without success. In reality, he was searching not just for a church but for God.

The fifteen-year-old Spurgeon had been brought up by Christian parents and grandparents, and he knew the Bible and Christian teaching inside-out. But somehow Christ still remained distant from him. In fact, for five years he had battled God. He had not committed, what would be considered, major sins, but his sins still seemed grievous to him. He believed that he had been given 'greater light' than most people, yet he still was a stranger to God's grace. He had no experience of salvation and no peace.

The wrath of God hung over him in the darkest of clouds. It seemed to hover there continually and he could not drive it from his mind. At that time 'ten black horses' pulled the plough that tore at his soul. Those ten horses were the ten commandments of God, and under them he knew he was condemned.

He trudged through the snow, the whiteness making everything look alike. He knew the area well and where all the local churches were, but in those conditions he could not find the one he was looking for. He was lost, yet he continued his search.

He eventually came upon a small, nondescript building. It was the Artillery Street Primitive Methodist Chapel. Primitive Methodism was a denomination that had separated from Wesleyan Methodism in 1811 and had grown quickly. It was energetically evangelistic and ministered mainly to the working class.

He entered the dark, unadorned building. The snow had partly caked the few windows that existed. The candles that flickered in the draughty chapel offered little by way of illumination.

There were only a few people in attendance but they welcomed their young visitor. A steward casually directed Spurgeon to a seat, though there were plenty to choose from, and the lad sat down. As Charles looked about him, he overheard a brief conversation between two of the men. 'I don't think Mr Platt's gonna make it in this weather, Joe. Not from where he lives. It looks like I'll have to preach.'

'Well, so be it, brother. You've done it before. God bless thee.'

The two men disappeared for a few minutes, reappeared and the volunteer went up the stairs to the pulpit. The service began with some vigorous singing. Few they may have been, but that did not impede the enthusiasm and energy of their worship. The Primitives had a reputation for doing everything loudly.

The makeshift preacher was tall and lean, and he bent over the pulpit as he read from the prophet Isaiah. There were calls of 'Amen' from the congregation but they were not always appropriately placed.

When the speaker stood up to preach, his lack of education was apparent. 'Look unto me, and be ye saved, all the ends of the earth,' he shouted. What he said was fine but it seemed to Spurgeon that each word was mispronounced. Then there was a silence, as if the preacher did not know what to say next.

Spurgeon remembered the rest of the text: 'For I am God, there is none else' (Isaiah 45:22).

At least that's a good text, thought Spurgeon. *A man could trust his life to that.*

It was soon obvious to Spurgeon that this man had little idea of how to preach. But the preacher was sure of his subject and he stuck with it. 'My dear friends, this is a very simple text indeed. It says, "Look!" Now lookin' don't take a good deal of pains. It ain't liftin' your foot or your finger; it's just "Look!" Well, a man don't have to go to college to learn how to look, he just looks. You may be the biggest fool but you can look. A man needn't be worth a thousand a year to look. Anyone can look. Even a child can look.' The short sentences were spat out with increasing rapidity.

'But the text says, "Look unto Me." Ay, that's right, it says, "Look unto *Me*." But many of you are looking unto yourselves. But it's no use lookin' there. You'll never find any comfort in yourselves. Some look to God, the Father. But no, look to Him by-and-by. Jesus Christ says, "Look unto Me" Some of ye say, "We must wait for the Spirit's workin'." But ye have no business to say that. Look to Christ. The text says, "Look unto me."

'"Look unto Me," says Christ. "I am sweatin' great drops of blood. Look unto Me, I am hangin' on the cross. Look unto Me, I am dead and buried. Look unto Me, I rise again. Look unto Me; I ascend to Heaven. Look unto Me; I am sittin' at the Father's right hand. O poor sinner, look unto Me! Look unto Me!'" The preacher's voice rose in pitch and volume as each clause was uttered.

Suddenly the man fell silent. He did not seem to know what to say next. He looked slowly around his tiny congregation and his gaze fixed firmly upon the young stranger in their midst. He pointed his finger at Spurgeon and directed his next comments at him. 'Young man, you look very miserable.'

Well, thought Spurgeon, *maybe I do but I am not accustomed to having remarks made from the pulpit on my personal appearance.* However, as Spurgeon later admitted, 'It was a good blow, which struck right home.'

But the preacher did not leave it there. He continued, 'And you will always be miserable—miserable in life and miserable in death—if you don't obey my text; but if you obey now, this moment, you will be saved.' Then lifting up his hands, he shouted at the top of his voice, 'Young man, look to Jesus Christ. Look! Look! Look! You have nothin' to do but to look and live.'

Spurgeon's eyes were suddenly opened. He 'saw at once the way of salvation'. As he later confessed, 'I had been waiting to do fifty things, but when I heard that word, "Look!" what a charming word it seemed to me. Oh! I looked until I could almost have looked my eyes away. There and then the cloud was gone, the darkness had rolled away, and that moment I saw the sun; and I could have risen that instant and sung with the most enthusiastic of them, of the precious blood of Christ, and the simple faith which looks alone to Him. Oh, that somebody had told me this before, "Trust Christ, and you shall be saved." Yet it was, no doubt, all wisely ordered.'

When Spurgeon later reflected on his life, he saw great value in his past experiences, however troubling they had been. He said, 'A spiritual experience, which is thoroughly flavoured with a deep and bitter sense of sin, is of great value to him that hath it.' Charles Haddon Spurgeon had long known the depths of guilt and despair. He had long suffered under a deep conviction of sin. But when he saw the Saviour and experienced His forgiveness, the joy became much greater than the despair had ever been.

CHAPTER 2

SPURGEON'S CHILDHOOD

Charles Haddon Spurgeon was born on 19 June, 1834, in the village of Kelvedon in Essex in the south-east of England. Haddon seems a strange name to give to a child, even as a second Christian name. It was not, as might be expected, the surname of a relative, but rather the name of a benefactor of his grandfather, Rev James Spurgeon. A Mr Haddon had shown great kindness to James Spurgeon, so the minister named one of his sons after him. Another son, Rev John Spurgeon, continued the tradition and gave his first child the names Charles Haddon. Thus Mr Haddon's kindness lived on in the name of one of the brightest lights in Christian history.

Eliza Spurgeon, the mother of Charles, was only 19 when he was born. Within a year she had given birth to another child. Soon after that, Charles was sent to stay with his paternal grandparents in nearby Stambourne, a village with a population of about 500. This was probably because Eliza was not well enough to care for two young children.

Grandfather James Spurgeon was the minister of Stambourne Congregational Chapel. James and his wife Sarah had served God in Stambourne for about 25 years and they were highly regarded by the local people. He was a man of great faith, a gifted preacher and his church was well filled each Sunday. He was also on good terms with those of other denominations, having a particularly friendly relationship with James Hopkins, the local evangelical Anglican rector.

James had an astute sense of humour, which his grandson inherited. He was rather stout and one day he had been asked, 'How much do you weigh?' He responded, 'Well, that depends on how you take me. If weighed in the balances, I am afraid I shall be found wanting *[Daniel 5:27]*, but in the pulpit they tell me I am heavy enough.'

James and Sarah had nine children, six boys and three girls. By now, they were well into their fifties and only three of their children remained at home: the 18-year-old Ann, James, about 15 and Susannah, about 12. 'Aunt Ann' took a major role in caring for her little nephew. She read him Bible stories, taught him to read and prayed with him and for him.

The manse was a large building, suitable in size to accommodate the Spurgeon family at its largest. But now, as the older children had moved away, there were unused rooms. The best room in the house was the parlour. Its walls were lined with the portraits of favoured ancestors. To the young Spurgeon, those ancient men seemed to peer down upon him and watch his every move.

Many rooms were left dark because of the 'window tax' imposed on home owners at the time. In those days the more windows you had, the more tax you paid, so the Rev Spurgeon, like many others, boarded up most of his windows.

Charles lived with his grandparents for five years and they became the foundation stone of his faith, understanding of Scripture and knowledge of church history. He often sat in the parlour as his grandfather prepared his sermons and was given strict instructions to keep quiet. Grandfather Spurgeon usually gave him the latest copy of the *Evangelical Magazine* to read, though in truth, in his early years it was well beyond his understanding. He did, however, take an interest in the few illustrations it contained, which usually included a portrait of a well-known clergyman and another of a missionary venture. Many years later, Charles Spurgeon's portrait took its turn on those pages.

Spurgeon learnt to read while very young. This meant that it was possible for him to read the Bible in family worship. One day the reading was from the book of Revelation, chapter 17. Charles read through to verse eight and stopped. The verse says that 'the beast … shall ascend out of the bottomless pit.' That presented a grave difficulty for the young boy. '*Surely,*' he thought, '*a pit, any pit, must have a bottom.*'

For a moment silence reigned. His grandfather was just about to ask him to continue when the lad burst out with, 'What does that mean, Grandfather? How can you have a "bottomless pit"?'

James Spurgeon was taken aback but was not inclined to answer. 'Not now, boy, not now. Go on with the reading.' So Charles finished the chapter.

The next day Charles chose the reading, selecting Revelation 17 once more. He read the first eight verses and stopped. Again he asked the meaning of 'the bottomless pit'. Grandfather Spurgeon again avoided answering and instructed his grandson to continue his reading.

But Charles wanted his answer. So the next day for a third time he read from Revelation 17. He did so again the following day and on the one after it. On each occasion, he repeated his question. James Spurgeon knew it was time to turn to other passages, but suspected that they were never going to move from that chapter until he had given a satisfactory response to the lad's question, so he did his best to answer it

'There is a deep pit', the old man began, 'and the soul is falling into it. Oh how fast it is falling. The last ray of light at the top has disappeared, and the soul still falls, on, on and on, and so it continues for a thousand years. Is it getting near the bottom? Will it stop? No! No! The cry is on, on and on. And so the soul goes on forever, falling into this bottomless pit. On and on forever!'

Charles was horrified, but he never forgot the lesson. The next day they read a different passage.

Charles also developed a love of nature. Birds used to nest outside his bedroom window, and much to his delight, a family of sparrows sneaked inside his room. The garden was large, the trees impressive, and it gave him great opportunity to fall in love with God's creation. Years later, this love of the natural world, God's world, would overflow in his sermons and books.

The boy's favourite room was what had once been a study. It was upstairs and was now windowless because of the tax. This made it too dark for its original purpose. However, it contained books— a whole treasure trove of Christian literature, including many written by the puritans. From this supply the young Spurgeon read Bunyan's *Pilgrim's Progress*, Foxe's *Book of Martyrs* and the many works of the puritans. In fact, Bunyan's allegory became, after the Bible, Spurgeon's favourite book. He read it many times.

When James Spurgeon hosted other clergy in his home, young Charles was allowed to sit in on the theological discussions. He did not remain a silent observer for long. At first he understood little, but he was quick to learn, and he soon showed that he had an excellent mind and the ability to comprehend deep truths. These discussions and his extensive reading gave him a comprehensive knowledge of the Bible, theology, church history and even how people thought.

Inevitably, Charles spent much time in the chapel, especially on Sundays. He heard his grandfather preach many times: grand sermons that they were. Members of the congregation had a strange way of praising their pastor's sermons. After the service some would come up to the preacher and say 'I heard you well this morning, Mr Spurgeon. I heard you well.' It is a good preacher who is heard 'well' by his congregation. But they were not the only comments that James received, for Charles remembered that some members could be critical of their pastor. Charles, with a flash of Spurgeon humour, later recalled that 'some were very wise in their remarks, and some were otherwise.'

On one occasion Charles noticed that his grandfather was grieving over the conduct of one of his congregation, who was making regular visits to the local tavern and drinking too much. Charles was moved by his grandfather's sorrow and decided to act. He marched to the pub, burst through the door and strode up to the man.

Charles pointed his finger at him. 'What doest thou here, Elijah?' he asked sternly. 'Here you are sitting with the ungodly, and you a member of a church and breaking your pastor's heart. I'm ashamed of you. I wouldn't break my pastor's heart, I'm sure.' With that the lad turned and walked out the door.

For a moment the man was dumbfounded. He was not used to having his conduct questioned, and the fact that it was a mere boy that was doing it made it even more stunning. When the man had recovered from the shock, he rose to his feet and left the pub, leaving his drink untouched. Later he apologised to James Spurgeon about his conduct.

***

The Spurgeon family was not musical. Consequently, James did not pay much attention to the musical side of worship in his church. He did compile a book of hymns he had written, but the standard was so poor that his grandson later said that he 'dare not quote even a verse'. To this day, they seem to have remained unquoted by anyone else.

The time came for Charles to leave Stambourne and return to his parents, who by this time, lived in the Essex town of Colchester; he did so with mixed feelings. He was sorry to leave the old man whom he loved dearly. On the day they parted they cried together. The wise old man in an effort to comfort the boy, told him, 'Now, child, tonight, when the moon shines at Colchester, and you look at it, don't forget that it is the same moon your grandfather will be looking at from Stambourne.' This impressed the boy so deeply that he could never look at the moon after that without thinking of his grandfather.

Fortunately, Charles was later able to visit his grandfather often and sometimes spent holidays with him. It appears that it was during one of these visits that Richard Knill, who had been a missionary in India, had visited Stambourne. Knill saw great potential in the young Spurgeon and spent considerable time talking to him, explaining the gospel and praying with him.

The missionary made a deep and lasting impression on the young lad. At one family prayer time, Knill sat Charles on his lap and predicted that the boy would preach to many thousands. At the time it seemed like a dream to Charles, but it was a dream that was to become reality. Spurgeon later called Knill's words from this time, 'a sort of star to my existence'.

On another visit to Stambourne, Grandmother Spurgeon offered Charles a penny for each Isaac Watts' hymn that he learnt off-by-heart. He memorised them so quickly and accurately that the poor woman became concerned about her household budget. She soon reduced the reward to a halfpenny and then to a farthing. Charles had a prodigious memory that served him well throughout his life.

There can be no doubt that the time Charles Spurgeon spent with his grandparents was a major influence upon his life. His early access to a wonderful library and his grandfather's mind helped form him into a great preacher of the gospel.

As to John Spurgeon, the father of Charles, though he was a preacher, he also had to work in a coal supplier's office to supplement the meagre family income. By the time Charles returned to his parents, there were three other children in the family and more were to come later. John

Spurgeon claimed 17 in all, though some almost certainly died in infancy.

John and his wife were prayerful people, and Eliza especially prayed for their obviously gifted, eldest son. Later Charles paid tribute to his 'praying, watching Mother'. On one occasion she had knelt beside Charles, with her arms around his neck, and prayed to God, 'Oh, that my son may live before Thee.' On Sunday evenings she would instruct her children in the Scriptures.

His first experience of school was in Stambourne, under the eye of 'old Mrs Burleigh'. He seems to have learned little from her, but was fascinated when he found out that her son's name was Gabriel.

'Is your son's name really Gabriel, Mrs Burleigh?' he asked.

'Well yes, my boy, it is.'

'Gabriel?' Charles asked again to make sure.

Mrs Burleigh nodded.

'I'd love to meet him, Mrs Burleigh. May I?'

'Well, I'll see what can be arranged.'

One day after school a most ordinary looking young man turned up. Mrs Burleigh introduced him. 'This is my son Gabriel, Charles.'

The young Spurgeon looked Gabriel Burleigh up and down. A frown creased Charles' brow. This Gabriel had no wings and there was nothing else especially angelic about his appearance. Charles was most disappointed. He politely shook hands, said, 'Please to meet you', turned and went home.

At about the age of ten, Charles went to Colchester's Stockwell School, at which he was usually top of the class or close to it. It seems to have been in his first year there that he won the school's First Class English Prize. He also did well in Latin and Mathematics. Clearly, his extensive reading had benefitted him in more areas than just theology and church history. This award surprised nobody, for he was always reading. While other children were playing, Charles was usually reading the latest treasure he had found in his father's library.

His younger brother James said, 'Charles never did anything else but study. I kept rabbits, chickens, pigs and a horse; he kept to books. While I was busy here and there, meddling with anything and everything that a boy could touch, he kept to books and could not be kept away from study. But though he had nothing to do with other things, he could have told you all about them, because he used to read about everything, with a memory as tenacious as a vice and as copious as a barn.'

His main teacher at Stockwell School was Mr Leeding, who, according to Spurgeon, was 'a man of prayer, faith, and firm principle'. Spurgeon also said that Leeding 'really taught his pupils' and it was his 'diligent skill' in teaching that helped Spurgeon form 'the foundation' upon which he later built.

Spurgeon later described himself in his childhood as 'a real careless, little fellow', who was always losing things. He was, for example, continually losing his pencils. Once he needed a new pencil but had no money to buy one. Christmas was coming, which should, he thought, solve the financial problem. But he needed the pencil right away. He entered the local shop and stood there feeling most uncomfortable.

'And what can I do for you, Master Spurgeon?' asked Esther Pearson, the kindly shopkeeper.

'I need a pencil, Miss Pearson.'

'Well, which one would you like? Take your pick.'

Charles stood there not quite sure whether he should go ahead with his plan, but he really needed that pencil. 'But I haven't got any money,' he said quickly.

'Oh!'

He hesitated for a few moments while he plucked up the courage to make a daring suggestion. 'But if I could have one now, I will be able to pay you after Christmas.'

'Well, my boy. That seems a good bargain. Take your pick and you can pay me when you get some money.'

'Oh, thank you, Miss Pearson. I am so grateful,' he said excitedly. He picked out a pencil, said thank you again and left the shop.

Charles Haddon Spurgeon was now in debt. It was only for the price of a pencil, it was true, but it was a debt nonetheless. This made him feel guilty. He did not dare tell his parents but somehow his father found out. So John Spurgeon took his son aside and gave him 'a very powerful lecture' about the dangers of debt. He then marched Charles down to the shop and paid the tiny amount owing, and gave him more warnings about not getting into debt. The young Spurgeon learnt his lesson. This was the only time in his life when he incurred a debt. Many years later he included a chapter against debt in his book *John Ploughman's Talk*, which began with a relating of this childhood experience.

At the age of 14, Spurgeon moved on to a Church of England school in Maidstone in Kent, where his teachers included Anglican clergymen. Once more he was the top of the class.

Surprisingly, it was through an incident at this school that he came to reject infant baptism. Both Congregationalism, his family's faith and the Church of England practised infant baptism. One day he was being instructed in the rite of baptism by one of the Anglican clergy. This minister told the boy that true baptism was only that which was administered by properly ordained Church of England clergymen. The baptism that Charles Spurgeon had experienced in a Congregational ceremony was invalid. Worthless!

Charles was shocked. 'But sir, my grandfather baptised me in our little parlour. He is a minister and a holy man of God, so I know he did it right.'

'Ah, my boy, but you had neither faith nor repentance, and

therefore you should not have been baptised.'

'But sir, that has nothing to do with it. All infants ought to be baptised.'

'But the Church of England Prayer Book says that faith and repentance are necessary before baptism, which is a scriptural doctrine. And in the Church the faith of an infant's parents or sponsors play that part, but this can't be so when baptism is conducted by dissenting ministers. Therefore your baptism was not a true baptism.'

Charles stood there in silence, which was rare for him.

'Think about it, my boy', instructed the clergyman. 'We'll discuss it again next week.'

So Charles went away and thought about it.

In the following week Charles also searched the Bible and came to the conclusion that his baptism as an infant in a Congregational Church was not a true baptism. Yet, in addition, he rejected the Anglican understanding of the rite, which he also regarded as unbiblical. Instead he came to believe that the Bible taught that baptism should only be administered to believers, so he became, in theory at least, a Baptist.

In August 1849, Charles moved from the school in Maidstone to another in Newmarket, Cambridgeshire. Strangely, one of the greatest influences on him at that school was the cook, Mary King. 'Cook', as she was known, was a Baptist, and though she had no formal theological education, she was a studious lady who took her faith seriously and read avidly.

The as-yet-unconverted Charles was drawn to her. She was, perhaps, the first Baptist he knew. They met together and shared insights on the Bible and theology, and it was Cook who did most of the teaching in these sessions. They discussed the deep truths of the Gospel, such as 'the covenant of grace, the personal election of the saints, their union to Christ, their final perseverance, and what vital godliness meant'. Many years later Spurgeon said, 'I learnt more from her than I should have learned from any six doctors of divinity of the sort we have nowadays.'

Charles Spurgeon was converted in January 1850 and was already in theory a Baptist. But he could be nothing just 'in theory'; he had to be the real thing. On 3 May 1850, his mother's birthday, he was baptised in the River Lark, near the Cambridgeshire village of Isleham. It was a blustery day and the water was cold, but Spurgeon did not mind. He was doing what he believed God required and that was enough.

Afterwards he declared, 'May I, henceforth, live alone for Jesus. I vow to spend my life in the extension of His cause.' He also said, 'Baptism also loosed my tongue and from that day it has never been quiet.'

From that day, it never was.

His parents were a little uneasy about his baptism but wisely decided to let him follow his own conscience. His mother, though, did offer a small protest. She said that when she prayed that God would convert her son, she did not pray that he would be made a Baptist. Charles responded, 'Ah, Mother, the Lord has answered your prayer with His usual bounty and given you exceeding abundantly above what you asked or thought.'

CHAPTER 3

THE BEGINNING OF HIS MINISTRY

Charles Spurgeon's first Christian ministry, two days after his baptism, was teaching in the local Sunday school. His own account of it runs, 'On a certain day, someone called – asked me – begged me – prayed me to take his class. I could not refuse to go. And there I was, held hand and foot by the superintendent and was compelled to go on. I was asked to address the children. I thought I could not, but no one else was there to do it, so I stood up and stammered out a few words.'

One suspects that Spurgeon's first attempt at teaching was not as bleak as he made it sound. Certainly, later the children listened to him intently. But their rapt attention caused him to speculate that this was because he was not much older than them. However, it was much more likely that it was because Spurgeon's style was simple and colourful, and they could understand him and relate to what he said. He also engaged frequently in the distribution of tracts.

At about the time Spurgeon had left Stockwell School, his teacher, Mr Leeding, also left and set up a school of his own in Cambridge. It was not long before Leeding invited his star pupil at Stockwell to assist him at this new school. This worked well for Spurgeon, for it not only gave him a source of income but he also continued to learn from Leeding.

He began to attend St Andrew's Street Baptist Church. On his first visit there he was disappointed because no one spoke to him. As he was leaving he said to a gentleman who had sat near him, 'I hope you are well, sir.'

The man gave him a puzzled look. 'You have the advantage of me. I don't know who you are.'

'I don't think I have any advantage, sir, for you and I are brothers.'

'What do you mean?'

'Well, when I took the bread and wine in the chapel just now, in token of being one in Christ, I meant it. Didn't you?'

The man blushed in embarrassment. 'You are right, young man, you are right', he said, placing his hands on Spurgeon's shoulders. 'You must come to tea with me.'

'When?'

'Well, now!'

So they trooped off to the man's house and shared a meal. They had not talked for long, before Spurgeon's companion realised that his new found friend was special. This boy seemed to know the entire Bible. In fact, he seemed to know almost everything. The next Sunday Charles Spurgeon was warmly welcomed into that church. On 3 October that year the church formally received him into its membership.

His first attempt at preaching was similar to his early Sunday school teaching. The lay-preacher's association of that area was led by James Vinter and he was always on the look-out for talented and spiritual young men to minister in the dozen or so churches in the area. Vinter recognised Spurgeon's ability and deep spirituality and he decided to send Charles to a nearby village to preach. However, because Spurgeon was so young, he thought that a direct appeal to him might not work.

'Master Spurgeon,' he said, 'a young man is going to preach at Teversham this Sunday. He is not much used to taking services, so why don't you go and help him?'

'I'd love to, Mr Vinter.'

'It's an evening service. The two of you should aim to arrive at five o'clock.'

'And who shall I be accompanying?'

'John Smith!'

'Oh!' Spurgeon knew Smith a little but he thought him a surprising choice for a preacher.

Vinter gave Spurgeon instructions to go to a certain cottage where the service was to be held. So on Sunday he met Smith and they began their walk to Teversham. As they walked, Spurgeon inevitably began a conversation.

'May I wish you every blessing as you preach today, brother John?'

Smith suddenly stopped. His feet seemed rooted to the spot, his face became ashen. 'Never! I'm not preaching. I can't preach. You are.' The words were spat out with emphasis. 'Mr Vinter just asked me to go with you to encourage you.'

Charles had now also stopped. For once he seemed lost for words. He looked back at his companion and the look of helplessness on his face. 'But I don't preach either.'

'But you teach in Sunday School. Preach one of your children's talks.'

'Yes, but …' Spurgeon's voice sunk into silence as he thought the problem through. He now realised that Vinter had tricked him into preaching, though, no doubt, with the best intentions. He, Charles Spurgeon, was to be the preacher for the tiny congregation at Teversham.

'Well, if that be so, we had better make our way then.'

They continued their walk, for the most part, in silence. John said nothing in case it might end up with him being asked to preach.

Charles was arguing with himself about what he should do. *Sunday School is one thing, but in Teversham I will be addressing adults. Probably nearly everyone will be older than me*, he thought. *Well*, he finally concluded, *surely I can tell a few cottagers about the sweetness and love of Jesus*. After that he felt a little more cheerful.

They arrived at their destination and Spurgeon still had not decided what text or what theme he would choose. His usual confidence had vanished.

Their host greeted the two young men and seemed by instinct to know which one was Charles. 'Ah, Master Spurgeon, it's so good of you to preach for us today.' He ushered them into the cottage. 'We're still expecting a few more but they should be here soon. We'll start as soon as you're ready.'

So Charles Haddon Spurgeon made himself ready and 'attempted to preach to the people'. He spoke from the text 'Unto you, therefore, that believe He is precious' (1 Pet 2:7). As soon as he began to speak his nervousness vanished. To Spurgeon, Christ was precious, and he found it easy to tell that to those poor folk. His listeners loved it and were deeply moved. They asked him to come back and preach again.

Later he recalled, 'I am sure I had no wish to do it – but there was no one else in the place. And should the congregation go away without a single word of warning and address? How could I allow it? I felt forced to address them.'

Charles Spurgeon was aware of a divine compulsion for him to engage in gospel ministry. He had to preach. His early reluctance and hesitancy were overcome by a force outside himself, or perhaps one should say, a divine force within him.

At the end of that first service one woman was bold enough to ask him his age. He replied, 'Under 60!' She responded, 'Yes, and under 16!'

Well before he had reached the age of 17, he was preaching at various chapels in the region, which he did with considerable enthusiasm. He made a great impact. People were delighted with his simple, yet challenging, messages and struck by his great spiritual power. Some were converted under his ministry. Many others were challenged to examine their lives in the light of the Word of God.

As he later reflected,

'I must have been a singular-looking youth on wet evenings, for I walked three, five, or even eight miles [5 to 14 kilometres] out and back again on my preaching work; and when it rained, I dressed myself in waterproof leggings and a mackintosh coat, and a hat with a waterproof covering, and I carried a dark lantern to show me the way across the fields. I am sure that I was greatly profited by those early services for my Lord. How many times I enjoyed preaching the gospel in a farmer's kitchen, or in a cottage, or in a barn! Perhaps many people came to hear me because I was then only a boy. In my young days, I fear that I said many odd things, and made many blunders; but my audience was not hypercritical, and no newspaper writers dogged my heels; so I had a happy training-school, in which, by continual practice, I attained such a degree of ready speech as I now possess.'

CHAPTER 4

MINISTRY AT WATERBEACH

'Mr Spurgeon is the minister of "the common people",' Rev John Anderson of Helensburgh.

Amidst all this busyness, the leaders at Waterbeach Baptist Church invited Spurgeon to preach at a Sunday service in October 1851. His sermon was on the text, 'Thou shall call his name Jesus, for he shall save his people from their sins' (Matthew 1: 21), which clearly showed the direction his ministry was taking. He was presenting Christ the Saviour to sinful men and women. He so impressed the small Waterbeach congregation that they soon asked this 17-year-old to become their pastor. He was now sure of the direction his life should take so he accepted the call.

Waterbeach is a Cambridgeshire village on an old Roman settlement, about ten kilometres from the city of Cambridge. It had a population of about 1,000 in Spurgeon's time. Like many other villages in England it was not a particularly moral place. Some of its residents engaged in the manufacture of illicit liquor; drunkenness and theft were common; and the rumour mill, probably not entirely inaccurate, hinted at what went on behind closed doors. It would be an exaggeration to say it was an especially wicked place, but nor was it noted for the godliness of its inhabitants.

When Spurgeon first became pastor of Waterbeach Baptist Chapel at the beginning of 1852, the congregation numbered about 40.

At first his salary was small, so he continued to teach in the school. However, Spurgeon made it clear that the moderate remuneration was not because his people were mean but rather because they were poor. However, the numbers at his church quickly increased, so they were able to pay him more and he was then able to leave school teaching and concentrate on the pastorate.

Word about the new Baptist pastor quickly spread, and more and more of the local community began to attend his church. As the news travelled further, people from neighbouring villages also began to pour into Waterbeach on Sundays to hear this wonderful boy preacher.

However, the chapel was too small to hold everybody. Over 400 arrived on some Sundays, so the doors and windows of the chapel were left open and those not able to gain a seat inside listened from outside, whatever the weather. His tender, yet powerful voice reached them all. Often he was also invited to preach in other churches on weekday evenings.

Spurgeon was always the evangelist. He understood the Gospel thoroughly, was clever with words, could speak dramatically and effectively, had an attractive personality, knew how to relate to people in groups or individually and most importantly was filled with the Spirit of God. It was not long before those who came only to hear a man, heard the Gospel he preached and responded to it. Converts were common.

Yet Spurgeon's preaching was not perfect. He, himself, knew it. Sometimes he worded his message too strongly or was a little too critical.

After one such occasion, a member of the congregation by the name of King took the unusual step of sticking a pin in Spurgeon's Bible next to a text he thought the young preacher needed to note. It read 'Sound speech that cannot be condemned; that he that is of the contrary part may be ashamed, having no evil things to say of you' (Titus 2:8). But Spurgeon quickly learned from his mistakes.

Soon after his arrival, a member of his congregation told him about the local 'nag'. This woman did not have a good word to say about anyone, and what she did say was usually spoken in highly colourful language. She had let it be known that the new minister would not escape her wrath; neither would he frighten or convert her.

Inevitably, one day she bumped into Spurgeon. The woman, knowing who he was, launched forth in an expletive-laden tirade about religion and the clergy.

Spurgeon smiled and said, 'Yes, thank you. I am quite well; I hope you are the same.'

The woman let loose again with another string of abuse.

Spurgeon smiled once more. He knew it was a waste of time trying to speak to her rationally, so he said, 'Yes, it does look rather as if it is going to rain. I think I had better be getting on,' and with that he turned and walked away.

For a moment the woman was lost for words. She then recovered herself and shouted after him, 'You're as deaf as a post.'

There is no known happy ending to that story. As far as Spurgeon knew she never attended his church or responded to the Gospel.

Spurgeon was already a preacher of the highest class but he also had a practical wisdom that aided him in helping others. He was a true and caring pastor as well as a great evangelist. A faithful woman in the Waterbeach congregation suffered from spiritual depression. She repeatedly complained that she doubted that she was saved. When she told Spurgeon of her doubts, he said, 'My dear friend, may I purchase your Christian hope for five pounds?' He put a hand in his pocket, as if to retrieve a bank note.

'Oh, no, Master Spurgeon,' she quickly responded, 'I would not sell my hope in Christ for a thousand worlds.'

Spurgeon smiled. The woman stood for a moment confused. Then a smile broke across her face and the doubts disappeared.

On one occasion, Spurgeon was invited to preach at the nearby village of Cottenham. The minister there had heard how good this new man was, so he invited him, sight unseen, to preach at their anniversary services.

Spurgeon arrived at the Cottenham chapel that Sunday morning and was directed into the vestry by an usher. 'Mr Sutton will be here in a moment,' the usher said. 'He will look after you.'

'Thank you; thank you so much.'

After a few minutes the aging Rev Sutton entered the vestry. He looked at Spurgeon and his mouth fell open in astonishment. '*You* are Mr Spurgeon?' he finally managed to say.

'Yes, Mr Sutton. I'm Charles Spurgeon. Thank you for inviting me to take your anniversary services. I regard it as an honour.'

Sutton looked Spurgeon up and down. He was not impressed. 'I wouldn't have asked you here had I known you were such a bit of a boy,' he said. He became silent for a few moments, standing with a forlorn look on his face, and then added, 'But the people have been pouring into the place all the morning in wagons, and dickey-carts, and all kinds of vehicles! I don't know what they are expecting. What kind of fools are they? All we have is a boy to preach to them.'

Spurgeon could not ignore the comment. 'Well sir, I suppose lots of people in attendance will make it so much the better for your anniversary. Still, I can go back as easily as I came, and my people at Waterbeach will be very glad to see me.'

'No, no,' said Sutton hastily, 'now you're here, you must do the best you can.'

When it was time for the service to begin Sutton directed Spurgeon to the pulpit. The elderly minister then sat on the pulpit stairs, as if ready to take over if Spurgeon broke down.

After prayer and singing Spurgeon read from Proverbs 16:31: 'The hoary head is a crown of glory.' Then he stopped mid-verse. 'Mind you I had cause to doubt that this morning. I met with a man who has a hoary head, yet he has not learnt common civility to his fellow-men.'

Sutton may have been the only person in the congregation who knew to whom the young preacher referred, but he felt himself turning red with embarrassment.

Spurgeon next read the whole of that verse, emphasising the second part. 'The hoary head is a crown of glory, if it be found in the way of righteousness.' He then continued with the service.

When he pronounced the benediction he came down the now empty pulpit stairs. For a moment Sutton was nowhere to be seen. Suddenly, he came up behind Spurgeon and slapped him on the back. 'Bless your heart, Master Spurgeon. I have been a minister nearly forty years, and I was never better pleased with a sermon in all my life.' Then he paused and a smile creased his aged face. 'But you are the sauciest dog that ever barked in a pulpit.'

It was the start of a close friendship. After Spurgeon came to know Sutton better, he thought of him fondly as 'a quaint old man'.

He was also invited to preach by the Baptists in Isleham. Their optimism was so great that they hired the largest hall in the town to hold the expected crowd. But only seven people turned up for the morning service. The organisers of that meeting were deeply embarrassed, but Spurgeon, who always gave his best, preached as if he were speaking to hundreds. He preached there again that evening and that time the hall was packed.

It was astonishing how one so young was able to master the arts of preaching and the wider pastoral ministry. It was as though he was born to preach. His brother James said that he leapt 'at a bound, full grown into the pulpit', and so he did.

Yet he had not had the college education that would normally be considered necessary before entering a ministerial career. Spurgeon was aware of this. His father was even more aware of it. So, with his father's persuasion, Charles went to meet with the principal of the Stepney College for training Baptist ministers. The arrangements were made, but Charles and the college principal were inadvertently directed to two different rooms in the same building and they did not meet.

After that, Spurgeon decided against attending the college. His father tried to persuade him to go but the boy had decided firmly against it. After all, he had attended two informal 'colleges' in the homes of his father and grandfather. It was not that he was against formal training for Baptist ministers, indeed, he later founded a college for that purpose, but rather that his biblical and theological training had been provided throughout his childhood. He was already thoroughly equipped for the work.

CHAPTER 5

NEW PARK STREET

In November 1853 Spurgeon spoke at a meeting of the Cambridge Sunday School Union. The meeting was not especially important in itself, but a gentleman by the name of George Gould was present and hearing the 19-year-old speak, he was deeply impressed. Gould had a friend named Thomas Olney. Olney was a deacon at New Park Street Baptist Church in London, just south of the Thames, which at that time was seeking a new pastor. Gould suggested that Olney consider Spurgeon.

The New Park Street Chapel had been opened in 1833, but the church that met there was considerably older. It had previously been on a different site and it was then known as Carter Lane Baptist. It had been a large and successful church. However, the New Park Street building was poorly situated and had an uninviting appearance. Spurgeon later said that it reminded him of the 'black hole of Calcutta'. Partly because of this, the congregation had declined considerably by the mid-19th century. While it could hold a congregation of 1,200, being one of the largest Baptist churches in Britain, there were usually less than 200 in attendance by the early 1850s.

Amongst its earlier preachers were Benjamin Keach (1640-1704), John Gill (1697-1771) and John Rippon (1751-1836). All, in their different ways, were highly regarded Baptist ministers. Keach was a leading figure in the early Baptist movement in England and was a prolific writer. In fact he was tried, found guilty and sent to the pillory for expressing Baptist beliefs in one of his books. Gill was a noted theologian with a number of important books to his credit, including commentaries on the Scriptures. Rippon had served in the ministry for over 60 years and had compiled a hymnbook that sold over 200,000 copies. It is said that John Rippon used to pray for the ministers, then unknown, who would follow him at New Park Street, that they would be used to increase its congregation significantly.

Though attendance at this church was fairly small in 1853, it still seemed absurd that a man not yet 20 should be considered to pastor it. Surely what was needed was someone with great ministerial experience to restore it to its former glories.

But on the last Sunday in November, Spurgeon went to Waterbeach as usual, and waiting for him was a letter inviting him to preach at New Park Street in December, with a view to becoming that church's pastor. With his knowledge of church history, Spurgeon knew a lot about that church. In fact, the Waterbeach Baptists used Rippon's hymnbook in their services. He was stunned by the invitation and at first thought it was a mistake. After all, why would a large and famous church call a 19-year-old?

He wrote back accepting the invitation to preach for them but expressing his surprise. He said,

'I have been wondering very much how you could have heard of me, and I think I ought to give some account of myself, lest I should come and be out of my right place. Although I have been more than two years minister of a church, which has in that time doubled, yet my last birthday was only my nineteenth. I have hardly ever known what the fear of man means, and have all but uniformly had large congregations, and frequently crowded ones; but if you think my years would unqualify me for your pulpit, then, by all means, I entreat you, do not let me come. The Great God, my Helper, will not leave me to myself. Almost every night, for two years, I have been aided to proclaim His truth.'

He soon received a reply that confirmed the invitation, setting the date of the 18 December.

On Saturday 17 December, Spurgeon arrived in London and the next morning preached at New Park Street. He must have been a shock to the congregation at first sight. He was of less-than-average height, deep-chested and a little overweight, with a round face and a head that seemed too large for his body. His youth was obvious, his clothes were quaint and being a country lad, he did not know how to behave in the big city.

But however much his appearance may have been out of place, his preaching hit the mark. His text was 'Every good and every perfect gift is from above, and cometh down from the Father of lights, with whom is no variableness, neither shadow of turning' (James 1:17).

He proclaimed God as 'a majestic figure', who is 'the father of lights'. The sun dims at night, is 'clouded' or 'eclipsed', but God is not like that: He is always light. 'The sun changes, the mountains crumble, the ocean shall be dried up, the stars shall wither from the vault of night; but God, and God alone, remains the same.' He is also the giver of 'every perfect gift'.

He closed by saying, 'I have succeeded in my object if, with me, you can from your hearts say, at the contemplation of Jehovah, "Glory be unto the Father, and to the Son, and to the Holy Ghost, as it was in the beginning, is now, and ever shall be, world without end. Amen!"'

The sermon was not intended to produce any particular effect, except to present 'the great I AM' to the people. However, it so excited those who heard it, that in the afternoon some visited their neighbours, friends and ex-church members, and invited them along to the evening service to hear this remarkable new preacher. Consequently, the attendance at the second service was much greater. This time Spurgeon preached on 'They are without fault before the throne of God' (Revelation 14:5). In this address he examined three things: firstly, 'the character of the people in Heaven', secondly, who the word 'they' represented, and thirdly, 'where' these people were, that is, 'before the throne of God'.

That evening the mood in the church was electric. As Spurgeon spoke, the Word seemed to become more dynamic, more alive. It struck home to minds and hearts with the power of the Holy Spirit. When Spurgeon finished, many seemed unwilling to leave. Some approached the deacons and urged them to call this young man to the pastorate of their church. But the deacons needed little persuading. They first invited Spurgeon to preach on three Sundays in January as a 'supply preacher'. Before January had reached its conclusion they called him to pastor the New Park Street church with a six month trial period, later reduced to three months at Spurgeon's suggestion. Few doubted the result of that trial.

The people of Waterbeach had known from the beginning of his ministry that Spurgeon would only be with them for a short time. He was too great a preacher to remain in a village church for long. It always seemed certain that a large London church would take him eventually, but all, including Spurgeon, were surprised it had happened so early. But even though they had expected him to leave sometime in the future, it didn't make their loss any easier to bear when it happened.

Spurgeon too, was sad to go. He had said in a letter to his father, 'I am contented where I am; but if God has more for me to do, then let me go and trust in Him.' He had made many friends at Waterbeach and he was sorry to bid them goodbye.

So at the age of 19, Charles Haddon Spurgeon began his ministry at New Park Street Baptist Church. It was to be a ministry that would impact the world.

Long before the planned trial period had been completed, the church held a business meeting that decided to offer Spurgeon the pastorate on a permanent basis. He replied, 'There is but one answer to so loving and cordial an invitation. I ACCEPT IT. I entreat you to remember me in prayer, that I may realise the solemn responsibility of my trust. Remember my youth and inexperience, and pray that these may not hinder my usefulness.'

Prayer was always a priority to Spurgeon. He prayed much himself, privately and publicly. What is more, he did not just *say* prayers, be they formal or informal, he really prayed. Yet prayer was not always easy for him. As a teenager he once complained, 'Prayer seems like labour to me; the chariot wheels drag heavily. Yet they are not taken off.' However, on a later occasion he said, 'How could I live without prayer when trouble comes?'

If at times prayer was difficult for him, as it is for us, it was always necessary, for trouble often came.

'Prayer is to me what the sucking of milk was to me in my infancy. Although I do not always feel the same relish for it, yet I am sure I cannot live without it,' he once said.

Arnold Dallimore said that in his public prayers Spurgeon 'talked with God in reverence but with freedom and familiarity'. He knew God as Saviour and Lord and revered him as such. But he also knew him as a loving Father and responded to Him as a loving son would. One of his contemporaries said, 'When Spurgeon prayed, it seemed as if Jesus stood right beside him.' Yet in the early days at New Park Street, a few did not approve of Spurgeon because they thought that he did not use 'sufficient reverence' in prayer. This probably meant that they thought that he spoke and behaved as though he was close to God.

But has not God in Christ made that possible? Spurgeon certainly thought so.

He did not believe in praying lengthy prayers. As he said, 'You cannot measure prayers by their length.'

With regard to prayer meetings, Spurgeon said, 'If a man will pray long, he may pray long somewhere else, but not at the meeting over which I preside.' Prayers could not be measured by their length. Rather it was the faith, passion and the Spirit within the prayers that made them powerful and effective. Many years later someone asked D L Moody, the great evangelist, whether he had heard Spurgeon preach. He replied, 'Yes, but better still I heard him pray.'

Spurgeon also sincerely desired his people to pray. He knew that the kind of ministry he was entering in London would be full of stress and difficulty. He felt that he needed a praying people to support him. And this is what he inherited.

From the time he arrived at New Park Street he realised his congregation prayed for him, and he was grateful to them for doing so. Within a year of his arrival, 500 regularly attended the church's prayer meeting.

Soon after he began his ministry at New Park Street, the deacons began to plan a service of ordination for their new pastor. However, Spurgeon protested in the strongest terms. To him, it was a meaningless ritual. He described it as 'placing empty hands on empty heads'. The ordination never took place.

From a few weeks after Spurgeon's arrival in London the New Park Street Church was regularly overflowing at the Sunday services and sometimes during the week as well. But crowds brought problems. As summer came on, it became hot inside the crowded church. Around the building were a number of windows, which gave light but no air, for they did not open. Spurgeon asked the deacons to have the glass removed from the separate upper part of each window to let in some air. The deacons were slow in responding.

One day an unseen villain smashed all these upper windows. Some members of the church were horrified by the vandalism but not Spurgeon. He said, 'A reward of five pounds shall be offered for the discovery of the offender, who when found, should receive the amount as a present.' As it turned out the one who smashed the windows was none other than Spurgeon himself.

Soon after his arrival in London, an outbreak of cholera struck the city. Cholera, originally observed in India, had arrived in Russia in 1823 and first hit England in 1831. The epidemic subsided within a year, only to re-emerge in 1848–49 and again in 1854. This latest outbreak was especially severe in London south of the Thames, where Spurgeon lived and served.

Inevitably, a number of people attached to his church contracted the disease. He visited them, even though it put his own life in danger. Some died, so funerals were frequent.

In a letter to his father at that terrible time he said that three members of his church had died on one day. He confessed to him, 'I do not know how to keep from constant weeping when I see others die.' His sensitive nature was tried by the suffering around him. 'Family after family,' he later wrote, 'summoned me to the bedside of the smitten and almost every day I was called to visit the grave'.

The heavy workload and the stress caused by the situation began to impact upon his health, though thus far, he had escaped the ravages of cholera. One day he was returning home from a funeral when he passed a cobbler's shop. In the shop window was a verse of Scripture, which said, 'Because thou hast made the Lord, which is my refuge, even the Most High, thy habitation; there shall no evil befall thee, neither shall any plague come nigh thy dwelling' (Psalm 91:9-10).

As Spurgeon read it 'Faith appropriated the passage as her own'. He remembered that at that moment he 'felt secure, refreshed, girt with immortality'. So he continued his visitation 'in a calm and peaceful spirit' and 'suffered no harm'. The epidemic abated and did not return until 1866.

When the 1854 outbreak of the disease had faded from the scene, Spurgeon and his deacons were able to concentrate on another problem. The church held 1,200 officially and hundreds more in reality, with many crowded into the aisles. But there were still many others who wanted to hear Spurgeon who had to be turned away because of the lack of room. So it was decided to enlarge the building.

During the 16 weeks that these alterations were being carried out in the first half of 1855, the church met at Exeter Hall in The Strand, north of the River Thames. Spurgeon's south London congregation had to cross the river during this period. Exeter Hall was a large building used for concerts and major functions of Christian groups. It seated about 4,000 and had standing room for another 1,000. Yet even this proved too small for all those wishing to hear him. Hundreds were turned away, but many refused to leave and congregated outside the hall, disrupting traffic.

One writer recorded his impressions of an evening service at Exeter Hall in some detail. He said,

'If the spectator has not taken care to enter before this time, he will have but small chance of finding even standing room. Suppose him to have entered early enough to have found a seat, he will naturally look around him to scan the features of the scene. They are remarkable enough to excite attention in the minds of the most listless. Stretching far away to the back are thousands of persons evidently eager for the appearance of someone. Towering up the platform, the seats are all crowded. Nearly all the eyes in this multitude are directed to the front of the platform. The breathless suspense is only broken occasionally by the struggle, in the body of the hall, of those who are endeavouring to gain or maintain a position.

Suddenly, even this noise is stopped. A short, squarely-built man, with piercing eyes, with thick black hair parted down the middle, with a sallow countenance only redeemed from heaviness by the restlessness of the eyes, advances along the platform towards the seat of honour. A cataract of short coughs, indicative of the relief afforded to the ill-repressed impatience of the assembly, announces to the stranger that the business of the evening has commenced. He will be told with a certain degree of awe, by those whom he asks for information, that the person just arrived is the Rev C H Spurgeon.'

Spurgeon, of course, was not entitled to the designation 'Rev' or 'Reverend'. He had not been ordained. But this did not stop him being called that, then and now.

To speak to such a vast assembly without mechanical aids was exhausting and had the potential to be a terrible strain on his voice. He kept a glass of chilli vinegar, which was usually used as a condiment, on a shelf under his makeshift pulpit. That was his short-term remedy for voice problems.

On one Sunday evening at the Exeter Hall he was preaching from the text, 'His Name shall endure forever' (Psalm 72:17). He preached that night with great passion, for it was a verse in which he delighted. As the sermon approached its conclusion, his voice began to tail off with hoarseness. Realising that he could not go on much longer, he made one final effort and drew his sermon to a hasty conclusion.

'Let my name perish,' he cried, 'but let Christ's Name last forever! Jesus! Jesus! Jesus! Crown Him Lord of all! You will not hear me say anything else. These are my last words in Exeter Hall for this time. Jesus! Jesus! Jesus! Crown Him Lord of all!' He then collapsed into the chair behind him.

Yet his voice survived. He used to say his throat was 'macadamised'.

It was so much used, yet survived the repeated ordeal. It was a God-prepared instrument.

The Sunday attendances of New Park Street Baptist Church had risen from less than 200 to around 5,000 in just a few months. Spurgeon, still only 20, had become one of the most popular preachers in London, if not the most popular.

One reason for the dramatic increase in attendances was because of personal recommendation. A significant example of this was from the actor Sheridan Knowles, who taught elocution to the students at the Regent's Park Baptist College.

He heard Spurgeon preach soon after the preacher had arrived in London. A few days later, when Knowles went to the college, he asked 'Boys, have you heard the Cambridgeshire lad at New Park Street?'

The students all looked back at Knowles with blank expressions on their faces. None of them had heard him.

'Then go and hear him at once if you want to know how to preach. His name is Charles Spurgeon. He is only a boy but he is the most wonderful preacher in the world. He is absolutely perfect in his oratory and a master in the art of acting. He has nothing to learn from me, or anyone else. He is simply perfect. He can do anything he pleases with his audience! He can make them laugh, and cry, and laugh again, in five minutes. His power was never equalled. Now, mark my word, boys, that young man will live to be the greatest preacher of this or any other age.'

But this 'success', if that is what it can be called, was a mixed blessing for Spurgeon. He rejoiced that thousands were coming to hear the Gospel and that many were being converted, but the awesome responsibility of his position at times overwhelmed him. In less than a year he had gone from being the pastor of a little-known country church to the pastor of a much larger church that had suddenly become one of the most popular in Britain. It was a weighty responsibility for a young man of 20 and sometimes that weight seemed to smother him. He later wrote,

> 'When I first became a Pastor in London, my success appalled me; and the thought of the career which it seemed to open up, so far from elating me, cast me into the lowest depth, out of which I uttered my *miserere*, and found no room for a *gloria in excelsis*. Who was I that I should continue to lead so great a multitude? I would betake me to my village obscurity, or emigrate to America, and find a solitary nest in the backwoods, where I might be sufficient for the things which would be demanded of me. It was just then that the curtain was rising upon my life's work, and I dreaded what it might reveal. I hope I was not faithless; but I was timorous, and filled with a sense of my own unfitness. I dreaded the work which a gracious providence had prepared for me. I felt myself a mere child, and trembled as I heard the voice which said, "Arise, and thresh the mountains, and make them as chaff." This depression comes over me whenever the Lord is preparing a larger blessing for my ministry; the cloud is black before it breaks, and overshadows before it yields its deluge of mercy.'

Charles Spurgeon often suffered from depression. This was partly because he was temperamentally disposed to it, partly because of the weight of the responsibility placed upon him from an early age, and in later life because of a number of physical ailments. Some argue that Christians should never be depressed but Spurgeon often was. This is one of the reasons he found such great comfort in the Psalms. He found in some of those mighty poems godly men who were brought to the edge of despair and were not afraid to show it, but still knew that God met them even there. He felt one with David and the other psalmists.

Spurgeon was, in fact, an emotional man. He often rejoiced but just as often felt downcast. This impacted upon his preaching. His sermons were intellectually solid but also deeply emotional. These were components that made him a great preacher. They helped him identify with those in the pews. Many came to church having suffered bereavements or job loss, or, on the other hand, had a newborn child or some triumph to celebrate. Spurgeon seemed able to meet the need of each one.

One day early in his ministry, an Irishman visited him. The visitor made a low bow and introduced himself.

'My name's Pat, your Riverence. I have come to ax you a question.'

'Oh!' Spurgeon responded, 'Pat, I am not a Riverence; it is not a title I care for but what is your question, and how is it you have not been to your priest about it?'

He said, 'I have been to him but I don't like his answer.' His brow creased with a frown.

'Well, what's your question?'

'God is just. That's right, isn't it? And if God be just, He must punish my sins. I deserve to be punished, don't I? Yet you say God is merciful and will forgive sins. I cannot see how that is right. He has no right to do that. He ought to be just and punish those who deserve it. Tell me how God can be just and yet be merciful.' The man's questions were sincere and asked earnestly.

Spurgeon replied, 'That's through the blood of Christ.'

'Yes, that's what my priest said. You are very much alike there. But he said a good deal besides that I did not understand. And that short answer does not satisfy me. I want to know how it is that the blood of Jesus Christ enables God to be just and yet to be merciful.'

Spurgeon thought for a moment. 'Now, Pat, suppose you had

killed a man and the judge had said, "That Irishman must be hanged".'

Pat interrupted. 'And I should have richly deserved to be hanged too.'

'But Pat, suppose I was very fond of you, can you see any way by which I could save you from being hanged?'

Pat thought for a moment. 'No, sir, I cannot.'

'Then, suppose I went to the Queen and said, "Please your Majesty, I am very fond of this Irishman. I think the judge was quite right in saying that he must be hanged but let me be hanged instead, and you will then carry out the law." Now, the Queen could not agree to my proposal, but suppose she could — and God can, for He has power greater than all kings and queens — and suppose the Queen should have me hanged instead of you, do you think the policemen would take you up afterwards?'

Pat quickly responded, 'No, I should think not. They would not meddle with me, but if they did, I should say, "What are you doing? Did not that gentleman condescend to be hung for me? Let me alone. Shure, you don't want to hang two people for the same thing, do you?"'

Spurgeon looked the Irishman in the eye, 'Ah, my friend, you have hit it; that is the way whereby we are saved! God must punish sin. Christ said, "My Father, punish Me instead of the sinner." And His Father did. God laid on His beloved Son, Jesus Christ, the whole burden of our sins, and all their punishment and chastisement. And now that Christ is punished instead of us, God would not be just if He were to punish any sinner who believes in the Lord Jesus Christ. If thou believest in Jesus Christ, the well-beloved and only begotten Son of God, thou art saved, and thou mayest go on thy way rejoicing.'

A look of understanding appeared on Pat's face and he clapped his hands. 'Faith, that's the gospel. Pat is safe now. With all his sins about him, he'll trust in the Man that died for him and so he shall be saved.'

Another of Spurgeon's early converts was a prostitute. She had reached a point of desperation and one Sunday evening had decided to go to Blackfriars Bridge and leap off it to her death. On her way she passed Spurgeon's chapel and, for reasons even she did not understand, entered and forced her way into one of the aisles. Once inside she began to doubt that she should be there. To her, everybody seemed too good and holy. But once she had entered it was impossible to get out.

Spurgeon's sermon that night was drawn from the text 'Seest thou this woman?' (Luke 7:44). It was about the woman, noted for her sinfulness, who washed the feet of Jesus with her tears and wiped them with her hair. As Spurgeon preached it seemed to the woman that he was speaking about her. She began to sob uncontrollably. That night she was saved twice. First, she was saved from committing suicide. Then she was saved 'from destruction' through faith in Jesus Christ.

In a similar incident, a man who frequently went to the gin-palaces was on his way home, customarily with a bottle of gin, when he passed New Park Street Church as the people were pouring in for a Sunday evening service. He suddenly had the urge to enter the church and followed the crowd up the steps to the gallery, pushing and being pushed as he went. He could not find a vacant seat, so stood at the back.

When Spurgeon preached he turned unknowingly in the man's direction and said, 'I think there is a man in the gallery tonight who has come into this chapel with the wrong motive.'

This comment, no doubt, could have referred to many in the congregation, but this visitor thought that it must refer to him. He was so shocked at what he perceived as a word directed to him that he listened carefully to the remainder of the sermon. By the end of the service the man was convinced of his guilt before God, and sought and found forgiveness in Christ.

The enlarging of the New Park Street Chapel only increased the seating to 1,500, with adjoining rooms fitted to seat a few hundred more. In the Exeter Hall Spurgeon had been preaching to about 5,000. Many who attended the services in that hall had not been previously associated with New Park Street, and some had not even associated with the Baptists. But many of these 'new' people wanted to continue hearing Spurgeon and made their way to the recently enlarged chapel. This meant that the space problem had not been resolved. It was still too small to hold all those wishing to attend its services.

A satisfactory solution to this problem was not quickly reached. In the end, the church's leaders decided to continue holding the Sunday morning services in New Park Street, but from 8 June 1856 they returned to Exeter Hall for Sunday evenings. This was not ideal but it had to do for the time being. The long term answer was to build a much larger church, but that would take time and money. The planning had already commenced.

Yet a cloud of bitter experience came to the minds of some. In the 1830s, the Scottish preacher Edward Irving had taken London by storm and a larger church had been built to house all those wishing to hear him. By the early 1840s, Irving had been dismissed from his church for allowing charismatic gifts in the services and from his denomination for suspected heresy. After he had gone, the services in the new building were not well attended, which limited its income, and the congregation found it difficult to pay off the debt.

Some were asking, 'Would that happen to New Park Street and Spurgeon?' But there was no hint of heresy with Spurgeon, and the crowds kept coming and growing.

At about this time Spurgeon had a striking experience in the pulpit, which, in part, foreshadowed the most difficult time of his life. One Sunday evening he had announced the hymn before the sermon and he opened the Bible to find the text from which he was to preach. Suddenly and unexpectedly, his eyes fell upon another verse upon the opposite page. This verse 'sprang upon' him 'like a lion from a thicket, with vastly more power than' he 'had felt when considering the text' he had originally chosen.

He later reflected, 'The people were singing, and I was sighing.' Which verse should he choose? The original text would be the safest. He had thoroughly prepared his sermon on that. But the other verse kept pounding through his brain. It seemed to cry out to him, 'You must preach from me! God would have you follow me.' As the people continued to sing, Spurgeon deliberated within himself as to which road to take. He thought, 'Well, I should like to preach the sermon that I have prepared, and it is a great risk to run to strike out a new line of thought; but still, as this text constrains me, it may be of the Lord, and therefore I will venture upon it, come what may.'

So he preached on the new text. He said that he 'passed through the first head with considerable liberty, speaking perfectly extemporaneously both as to thought and word. The second point was dwelt upon with a consciousness of unusual quiet, efficient power.' But at that stage he had no idea what his third point would be.

Before he could summon his thoughts to tackle the next part of the sermon all the gas lights went out. They were in darkness. Spurgeon immediately sensed the danger. The church was packed, with people even sitting in the aisles. If anybody panicked a nasty situation could develop. A murmur of concern arose from the congregation.

What should he do? He still had no third point, but at least he was not relying on hand-written notes, which would now be unreadable. He first urged the people to stay calm and remain in their seats, and assured them that the lights would soon be relit.

He then turned his sermon on to a different track, referring to a number of Bible verses on light and darkness. As he spoke, he developed his theme and various illustrations sprang into his mind.

Then the lights were relit and Spurgeon gazed out into his audience, which was 'as rapt and subdued as ever a man beheld in his life'.

A few weeks later Spurgeon heard that two people had been converted during that service, one in the first part of the sermon and the second when he redirected his thoughts after the lights went out. He later reflected. 'Thus providence befriended me. I cast myself upon God and His arrangements quenched the light at the proper time for me. Some may ridicule, but I adore; others may even censure, but I rejoice.' Added to that, what could have been a dangerous situation passed without trouble.

The remarkableness of Spurgeon's early ministry was not just the massive crowds he attracted, but the number who were touched by Christ through his preaching. Many of his hearers came under conviction of sin and needed spiritual guidance. He spent an hour each Monday and Thursday evening specifically dealing with enquirers. But there were so many that even though he gave each only a brief interview, he was unable to see all those wishing to speak to him. Spurgeon told a friend at this time, 'Friends firm. Enemies alarmed. Devil angry. Sinners saved. Christ exalted. Self not well.'

Spurgeon knew that God was with him in all things big and small. One day, when he was returning by train from a preaching engagement in the country, he suddenly realised that he had lost his ticket. The problem was made worse by the fact that Spurgeon had no money on him. No ticket and no money to pay the fare at the other end. He was fumbling in his pocket, unsuccessfully searching for the ticket, when a man, the only other occupant in that carriage, asked, 'I hope you haven't lost anything, sir?'

Spurgeon thanked the man and told him that he had lost his ticket. 'But', said, Spurgeon, 'I am not at all troubled, for I have been on my Master's business, and I am quite sure all will be well. I have had so many interpositions of Divine providence in small matters as well as great ones that I feel as if, whatever happens to me, I am bound to fall on my feet.'

The man smiled and the two engaged in conversation until the train had nearly reached Spurgeon's destination. Then the ticket collector came round for the tickets. The collector opened the door of the compartment and he touched his hat to Spurgeon's travelling companion.

Spurgeon's new found friend said to the railway man, 'It's all right, William.' And the ticket man again saluted him and left the compartment.

'That's strange,' said Spurgeon to the other man. 'The ticket collector did not ask for my ticket.'

'No, Mr Spurgeon,' he said, showing recognition of the preacher for the first time. 'It's another illustration of what you told me about the providence of God watching over you even in little things. I am the General Manager of this line, and it was no doubt divinely arranged that I should happen to be your companion just when I could be of service to you. I knew you must have bought a ticket. It has been a great pleasure to meet you under such happy circumstances.'

The man reached out, shook Spurgeon's hand and then climbed down from the train. Spurgeon sat stunned for a moment, smiled and then he too disembarked.

CHAPTER 6

SUSANNAH

A young lady named Susannah Thompson had been present on the
first evening that Spurgeon had preached at New Park Street, back in
December 1853. She later reflected,

> 'I was not at all fascinated by the young orator's eloquence,
> while his countrified manner and speech excited more regret than
> reverence. I was not spiritually minded enough to understand his
> earnest presentation of the Gospel, and his powerful pleading
> with sinners, but the huge black satin stock [a type of scarf],
> the long, badly-trimmed hair and the blue pocket-handkerchief
> with the white spots attracted most of my attention, and, I fear,
> awakened some feelings of amusement.'

It was not love at first sight.

Susannah's parents were friends of the Olney family. They often
exchanged visits to each other's home. Charles Spurgeon was another
common visitor to the Olney residence. Inevitably, Charles and Susannah
met informally on some of these occasions. They also met at church.

On 20 April 1854, soon after he had settled in London, he gave
her a copy of Bunyan's *Pilgrim's Progress*, inscribed with 'Miss
Thompson with desires for her progress in the blessed pilgrimage' and
signed, 'From C H Spurgeon'. It was well intended, though formal,
and probably had more to do with concerns about her spiritual standing
than a step towards courtship.

Spurgeon, as far as is known, had had no romances so far. His life had been filled with study and work and he had little time to spend looking for a wife. But now matters began to move in that direction. At meetings at church and at the Olney home they began to learn more about each other.

Susannah, usually known as Susie, confessed that though she had become a believer sometime before, she had slipped backwards in her faith, while still observing the Christian formalities. But it was hard to remain in a complacent backslidden condition for long when you had close contact with Charles Spurgeon. He would either inspire you to a closer walk with God, or convince you to be somewhere else. As it happened, Spurgeon's preaching and the conversations they had reinvigorated her faith.

About two months after his settlement in London, Charles and Susannah went to the reopening of the Crystal Palace with some friends from the church. The Crystal Palace had been built in 1850 for the Great Exhibition, which had been a major triumph for Britain. The iron and glass building had then been pulled down and rebuilt in Sydenham not far from where they lived, and it was reopened in June 1854.

As has been seen, Spurgeon was an ardent reader, and even though he was at a grand event with a group of friends, it did not stop him from taking a book with him. Indeed, he read it during the quieter moments of the day. As events proceeded, he leant over to Susannah and showed her a section in the book about marriage and asked her what she thought of it.

'Seek a good wife of thy God, for she is the best gift of His providence. Yet ask not in bold confidence that which He hath not promised. Thou knowest not His good will. Be thy prayer then submissive thereunto, and leave thy petition to His mercy, assured that He will deal well with thee. If thou art to have a wife of thy youth, she is now living on the earth. Therefore think of her and pray for her weal [her welfare].'

He then whispered in her ear, 'Do you pray for him who is to be your husband?'

This was a startling and unexpected question under the circumstances. Susannah was struck dumb by it. However, though her voice was silent, her mind was racing and her heart was pounding.

When the pageantry was over, Charles once more leant over to Susannah and said, 'Will you come and walk around the palace with me?' She nodded her acceptance. Then, amidst the crush of people, they managed to untangle themselves from their friends and took their walk around the various exhibits and gardens.

While it had not been love at first sight, love had now entered their relationship.

Less than two months later, Charles and Susannah visited her grandfather. As they walked around the old man's garden hand-in-hand, Charles poured out words of love to her and asked her to marry him.

For a moment Susannah was silent, but it was not because of any doubts about how she would answer. Rather it was silence induced by excitement. As she later said, she was 'silent for very joy and gladness'.

The answer, of course, was 'yes'. After they parted that day she went to a private room in that house, 'knelt before God, and praised and thanked Him, with happy tears, for His great mercy in giving [her] the love of so good a man'. That evening she wrote in her diary, 'It is impossible to write down all that occurred this morning. I can only adore in silence the mercy of my God, and praise Him for all His benefits.'

But the formalities still had to be observed and parental permission was asked and given.

Spurgeon began to meet with his wife-to-be on Monday mornings but it was not private or particularly romantic. By this time he was a major figure on the Christian landscape and there was a great call for his sermons in print. He would preach a sermon on Sunday and edit it on Monday morning, so that it could be collected for printing that afternoon and distributed on Thursday for the Spurgeon-hungry public. Their private time had to be fitted into the demands of his duty. In fact, preparing his sermons for printing became a common labour for Spurgeon throughout his life. The demand for his printed sermons increased rapidly, and they are still distributed and read today.

Susie and Spurgeon often met at the Crystal Palace on Friday afternoons. Charles found the city oppressive, and he liked to saunter around the gardens and displays at the Crystal Palace to gain some relief. The church also held a prayer meeting each Thursday evening, which both Charles and Susie attended. After the meeting closed he would meet her in one of the aisles and say, 'Three o'clock tomorrow?' She nodded and they had met.

If Susie's faith had been weak early in 1854, it strengthened considerably in the second half of that year. On 1 February 1855 her fiancé baptised her. As part of this process she had to 'come before the church' and give an account of her spiritual experience. There were several candidates for baptism on that occasion. One baptised before her was an elderly man named Johnny Dear.

When he had told of his Christian experience a lady at the back of the church leant over and said to her friend, 'And what was his name then?'

Her companion replied, 'Johnny Dear!'

'Oh, and I suppose it will be Susie Dear next.' And it was.

The relationship between Charles and Susie did not always run smoothly. On a few occasions she would enter the vestry when he was preparing to take a service and he would shake her by the hand as if she were a stranger, then suddenly realise his mistake and ask her to forgive him. This was especially strange because Spurgeon had a remarkable memory for names and faces.

He was often invited to preach at other denominations' chapels and at major events in a variety of large halls, though more often than not he had to refuse because he received so many invitations. On one occasion he and Susie travelled together to one venue in a cab. They entered the building and Charles, his mind set on his sermon, forgot his fiancée. They became separated in the crowd. He went with his host, while Susie was left behind. What was worse, he seemed unaware of the fact.

Understandably, she was not impressed. She was a strong-willed young lady and did not take kindly to such treatment. As she later said, at first she was 'utterly bewildered' and then '*angry*'. How could the man she loved and who said he loved her, treat her so? She quickly got a cab back home and was greeted by her surprised mother. Her mother comforted her, but counselled that as her fiancé was a man with unique talents and so dedicated to God and His service, it would be a mistake to expect to always have his attention. Susie already knew this but it was not easy to work it out in practice.

Later that evening a greatly stressed Charles Spurgeon arrived in a cab at the Thompson residence and knocked feverishly on the door. Mrs Thompson opened it.

'Where's Susie?' he cried. 'Where's Susie? I have been looking for her everywhere and can't find her. Has she come home?'

Mrs Thompson thought it best to explain to him what had happened before the two lovers met with each other. She sat him down in the parlour and told him that Susie had been most upset that he had neglected her. She also told him about the words of counsel she had given to her daughter.

This succeeded in making Charles even more emotionally wrought. He had distressed the woman he loved and he deeply regretted it.

Mrs Thompson went to get Susannah, brought her into the parlour where Charles waited, and wisely left the two alone. For a few moments there was great tension. Neither knew how to express their feelings. Then Susie poured out her heart to Charles, telling him how he had hurt her.

Charles listened quietly, his face etched with anguish.

When she had finished he moved over to her, took her hand and with tears in his eyes, apologised. 'Susie,' he said, 'I am so deeply sorry. I love you more than any other person on earth. You know that I do. I am sorry that I hurt you. But your Mother is right. God comes first, and sometimes I am so intent on doing His work, I forget everything else. I did not mean to hurt you and I will try to be more careful in future. But Susie, never forget that I love you.'

They had both learnt a lesson that day but it had been an especially hard lesson for her. It is difficult for the wives of famous men (or the husbands of famous women) to cope with the demands placed upon their spouses and the interference that brings to private and family life. Susie was now in that situation. She coped by remembering that God's work was the most important, and that her husband gave so much time and effort to it, did not mean he loved her any less. Learning that lesson meant she enjoyed him all the more when they were alone.

Some years later he wrote her a poem, which called her 'the joy of my life'. The last stanza reflected the lessons both had learnt.

Though He who chose us all worlds before,
Must reign in our hearts alone,
We fondly believe that we shall adore,
Together before the throne.

They were married on Tuesday 8 January 1856 at the New Park Street Chapel. Early that cold and cloudy day, a crowd began to assemble outside the church. Though it was a weekday, well before the commencement of the service, thousands were jostling each other in the street outside. The police were on hand to control the crowd but it is impossible to control thousands when they are trying to fit into a space too small for them all. Eventually, the church was filled, but many still stood in the streets outside. Dr Alexander Fletcher, the elderly pastor of Finsbury Chapel, conducted the service.

After the wedding it was the honeymoon in Paris. France was to become an important part of Spurgeon's later life.

That September they moved to a new home, Helensburgh House. Ten days later, Susannah gave birth to twin boys, Charles and Thomas. They were to be their father's delight.

CHAPTER 7

OPPOSITION

When hell, enraged, lifts up her roar,
When Satan stops my path before,
When fiends rejoice and wait my end,
When legion'd hosts their arrows send,
Fear not, my soul, but hurl at hell
Thy battle-cry, Immanuel. (C H Spurgeon)

Letters requesting that Spurgeon preach in different places kept coming from, as he put it, 'here, there and everywhere'. It was impossible for him to fulfil all the many requests. In the middle of 1855, he went on a preaching tour of the north of England and Scotland, and spoke in numerous crowded chapels and halls. So great were the numbers clamouring to hear him that many had to go away disappointed.

Strangely in Scotland, the secular press praised him, while the *Christian News* criticised him. The latter spoke of his 'buffoonery' and told of 'a respectable audience' being 'amused, or disgusted, in Hope Street Baptist Chapel' on the first Sunday morning after his arrival. It then complained about him flinging out 'platitudes and stale anti-Arminianisms to a large audience in West George Street Chapel' that evening. In another edition the *Christian News* called Spurgeon 'a spoiled boy, with abilities not more than mediocre'. Yet the people still came to hear him in their thousands, with many unable to gain entrance into crowded churches.

But amidst the success that would have thrilled most preachers, there were still times when he was down. He told Susie in a letter 'I preached in Edinburgh, and returned here, full of anguish at my ill-success. Ah! my darling, your beloved behaved like Jonah, and half wished never more to testify against Nineveh. Though it rained, the hall was crowded, and there was I without my God! It was a sad failure on my part; nevertheless, God can bless my words to poor souls.' No doubt, matters were not as bad as he had painted them, but sometimes the 'black dog' of depression bit him deeply. And being away from Susie did not help.

Spurgeon also preached in the open air on occasions. In one instance in the summer of 1855, he preached to an estimated 10,000 in Hackney in London's East End, and when he left the people cheered him.

He later reported:

'After the service, five or six gentlemen endeavoured to clear a passage, but I was borne along, amid cheers, and prayers and shouts, for about a quarter of an hour. I was hurried round and round the field without hope of escape until, suddenly seeing a nice open carriage, with two occupants, standing near, I sprang in and begged them to drive away. This they most kindly did, and I stood up, waving my hat, and crying, "The blessing of God be with you!" While from thousands of heads the hats were lifted, and cheer after cheer was given. Surely, amid these plaudits I can hear the low rumblings of an advancing storm of reproaches; but even this I can bear for the Master's sake.'

Charles Spurgeon was very popular. But he was also unpopular amongst certain groups. The 'low rumblings' he could hear were to rise in volume.

Though thousands adored him and listened to him avidly and

read his sermons, there were plenty who criticised him savagely. In 1856, his publishers Joseph Passmore and James Alabaster said, 'The tongue of the wicked has assailed Mr Spurgeon with the most virulent abuse and lying detraction. His sentiments have been misrepresented and his words perverted. His doctrines have been impugned as "blasphemous", "profane" and "diabolical".' Some of the criticisms were flippant, others were more pointed or theological and potentially more damaging.

Jesus said, 'Blessed are ye, when men shall revile you and persecute you, and shall say all manner of evil against you falsely, for my sake. Rejoice and be exceeding glad; for great is your reward in Heaven; for so persecuted they the prophets which were before you' (Matthew 5:11-12). On that basis, Spurgeon must have been blessed.

For example, a correspondent in the *Ipswich Express* claimed that Spurgeon had 'had the impudence' to advise the young ladies in his congregation from the pulpit that, as he was engaged, 'he wanted no presents sent to him, no attentions paid him, no worsted slippers worked for him'. A number of people responded saying that the claim was false and then that newspaper published a retraction. But the damage was done. Other papers picked it up. The *Lambeth Gazette* said, 'The young sisters are dancing mad after him. He has received slippers enough from these lowly-minded damsels to open a shoe-shop.' In addition, the *Empire*, a London paper, and the *Christian News* of Glasgow also reported it.

There can be little doubt that when he arrived at New Park Street many young ladies in Spurgeon's congregation were attracted to him (Susie Thompson excepted, it seems). This is the common lot of young, unmarried ministers in sizable churches. However, there is no evidence that he received numerous pairs of slippers from his female admirers, and it was denied by members of the New Park Street congregation that he stated from the pulpit that he wanted no more gifts from them.

With regard to his standing as a preacher, the fact that he had not been to a training college went against him. Some automatically thought that this must mean his teaching was either false or inadequate or both.

Others thought him too flamboyant. One Congregational minister (from the denomination in which Spurgeon had been raised) thought his preaching 'an insult to God and man'. A journalist said that 'All his discourses are redolent of bad taste, are vulgar and theatrical.' A letter in an Essex newspaper described 'his style' as being 'that of the vulgar colloquial, varied by rant'. It added that 'His rantings are interspersed with course anecdotes that split the ears of groundlings.'

The same letter reported that his preaching contained 'low views of Deity', while 'All the most solemn mysteries of our holy religion are by him rudely, roughly and impiously handled. Mystery is vulgarised, sanctity profaned, common sense outraged and decency disgusted.' Another paper called his sermons 'dogmatic theological dramatising', 'outrageous manifestations of insanity' and 'ginger-pop sermonising'.

Another letter that appeared in a newspaper called Spurgeon's preaching 'a prostitution of the pulpit', while one prominent fellow minister accused him of preaching 'a half-way gospel' and doubted that he had been genuinely converted. The *Daily Telegraph* called him 'a ranting charlatan', who took people 'by the nose' and bullied 'them into religion'.

Another letter writer accused Spurgeon of 'exhibiting that matchless impudence, which is his great characteristic, indulging in coarse familiarity with holy things' and 'declaiming in a ranting and colloquial style'. This writer also blamed him for 'strutting up and down the platform as though he were at the Surrey Theatre and boasting of his own intimacy with Heaven with nauseating frequency'. He added, 'I have glanced at one or two of Mr Spurgeon's published sermons, and turned away in disgust from the coarse sentiments and clap-trap style.' Indeed, the sermons of this 'nine days wonder' are 'trashy'.

In 1857 Spurgeon said, 'I cheerfully accord to all men the liberty of abusing me. But I must protest against the conduct of at least one editor, who has misquoted in order to pervert my meaning, and who has done even more than that; he has manufactured a "quotation" from his own head, which never did occur in my works or words.'

Spurgeon was also criticised for being critical of others. In September 1855 the *Patriot*, a paper with Congregational Church backing, argued 'All, in turn, come under the lash of the precocious tyro. He alone is a consistent Calvinist; all besides are either rank Arminians, licentious Antinomians, or unfaithful professors of the doctrines of grace.' Yet oddly, he was also accused of trying to appeal to people of differing theological persuasions.

But while Spurgeon certainly criticised others, especially in his early days, his criticism was not as unreasonable, unkind or as widespread as some suggested. He did, for example, praise some Methodists, even though he rejected their Arminian doctrine. After all, he had been converted in a Primitive Methodist chapel. In fact, he called John Wesley a 'good man' and Methodism 'a great denomination'. On one occasion he quoted the Apostles' Creed, saying, 'I believe in the communion of saints' and added, 'I do not believe in the communion of Baptists only.' To Spurgeon the communion table in his church should be open to all believers, not just Baptists.

Some accused him of being a Hyper-Calvinist, whilst others called him an Arminian. Yet he could not be both. In fact, he was a genuine Calvinist, believing in God's predestination of only some to salvation, whilst insisting that the Gospel should be preached to all. After all, he did not know who was predested. He rejected Arminianism, loved 'glorious Calvinism', but said that Hyper-Calvinism was 'too hot for [his] palate'.

It would be a mistake to think that this criticism did not hurt Spurgeon. He felt it deeply, especially early on, but he did not let it destroy him. He had found the criticisms 'galling enough' early in his career, but he said that later he 'grew inured to falsehood and spite'. He also said, 'We should learn to be despised, learn to be condemned, learn to be slandered, and then we shall learn to be made useful by God. Down on my knees have I often fallen, with the hot sweat rising from my brow, under some fresh slander poured upon me. In an agony of grief, my heart has been well-nigh broken; till at last I learned the art of bearing all, and caring for none.'

After being called 'vulgar' by one journal he responded, 'I am, perhaps, "vulgar" and so on, but it is not intentional, save that I *must* and *will* make the people listen. My firm conviction is that we have quite enough *polite* preachers, and that "the many" require a change.' His language was vivid but not vulgar, and if some thought it so, it was their judgement that was at fault, not Spurgeon's language.

He told Susie in a letter, 'I am down in the valley, partly because of two desperate attacks in *The Sheffield Independent* and *The Empire*, and partly because I cannot find a subject. Yet faith fails not. I know and believe the promise, and am not afraid to rest upon it. All the scars I receive are scars of honour; so, faint heart, on to the battle! My love, were you here, how you would comfort me, but since you are not, I shall do what is better still: go upstairs alone, and pour out my griefs into my Saviour's ear. "Jesus, Lover of my soul", I can to "Thy bosom fly!"'

In a separate letter he told her, 'The devil has barked again in *The Essex Standard*. It contains another letter. Never mind; when Satan opens his mouth, he gives me an opportunity of ramming my sword down his throat.'

The Saturday Review was particularly strong in its criticism. It dubbed him 'a very ordinary imposter' and 'a coarse, stupid irrational bigot'. This caused Spurgeon to bark back that the true Christian 'is one who fears God and is hated by *The Saturday Review*', and some of Spurgeon's supporters began to call that paper the 'Satanic Review'.

Many, of course, came to his defence or praised him. For example, *The Patriot* had 'a glowing account' of him, which he feared 'would make him more popular than ever'. He prayed that God would preserve him amidst this adulation. He even said, 'all my little troubles have just kept me right. I should have been upset by flattery, had it not been for this long balancing rod' of criticism. He also said, 'It is not for me to take either praise or censure from man, but to stand independently upon the solid rock of right doing.'

Charles Haddon Spurgeon was now not just a preacher of the Gospel, but a highly controversial figure.

CHAPTER 8

THE TRAGEDY

When storms of sorrow toss my soul,
When waves of care around me roll,
When comforts sink, when joys shall flee,
When hopeless gulfs shall gape for me
One word the tempest's rage shall quell,
That word, Thy name, Immanuel. (C H Spurgeon)

It often happens that criticism of a person attracts others to their cause, or at least draws them to make judgement for themselves. This happened to Spurgeon. Publicity, even bad publicity, made more people want to hear him. But the New Park Street Church was too small to hold them. Even the Exeter Hall was too small and anyway, those responsible for it were reluctant to hire it out to one denomination for a lengthy period.

It was clear that the building at New Park Street could never be made large enough to hold all those wishing to hear Spurgeon, so a new church must be erected. In June 1856 a committee was established to set about planning a new, much larger building. But what could they do in the meantime?

Spurgeon and his church leaders began to consider using the Surrey Gardens Music Hall. The Surrey Gardens Hall was a massive building reputed to hold over 10,000. Surrey Gardens was originally a large garden open to the public, complete with a zoo. Its popularity declined after the opening of the Crystal Palace, so it was sold and the new owners built what was believed to be the largest public auditorium in Britain. It had a long area on the ground floor, with three extensive galleries.

But could Spurgeon preach to a crowd that size? Would his powerful voice reach all in such a vast assembly? Whitefield, a century before, was said to have preached to over 30,000 in the open air, though in reality it may have been half that, and only in favourable conditions could he be heard by all. Could Spurgeon do that indoors? He would have no mechanical aids to help him. It would just be the power of his voice. In addition, preaching to such a large assembly was a great responsibility, which Spurgeon would take to heart, and with his temperament, it was always likely to be a highly emotional rollercoaster ride.

The decision was made. They hired the hall and the first service was planned for Sunday evening 19 October 1856. It was a tremendous opportunity but Spurgeon was uneasy.

On that day the people began to assemble outside the hall from around noon. When the doors were eventually opened the crowd flooded in, occupying every seat and filling the aisles and occupying the stairwells. The expected crowd of 10,000 had become considerably more and still thousands gathered outside trying to get in.

When Spurgeon arrived he saw the great crowd milling about outside the hall and was stunned by its size.

'So many people!' he said to a companion.

'Yes, and those are the ones that can't get in.'

'Can't get in?'

'Yes! The hall is already full!'

Spurgeon felt his stomach churn.

He was directed to a small room to the side of the main auditorium, which was being used as a vestry. As he waited for the time the service was to commence, he felt nauseous. This was quite common for him, but on this momentous occasion the affliction seemed worse than it usually was.

The deacons joined him for prayer and then Spurgeon entered the great auditorium. He was overwhelmed. Before him was a vast sea of faces, stretching from near where he would preach right to the rear of the building. As he glanced up he saw that the galleries too were full. It was a formidable mass of humanity. He hesitated for a moment, then recovered and began by announcing the first hymn, which was sung with great enthusiasm and at a considerable volume. After that he felt a little better. The service continued in the normal way, he prayed, read from the Bible, they sang another hymn and Spurgeon prayed the pastoral prayer. He closed that with 'Amen!'

Then it happened.

'Fire! Fire!'

Immediately there was a stir.

'The galleries are falling.'

People began to rise from their seats.

'The building is collapsing.'

More rose from their seats and tried to make haste to the aisles. But the aisles were already packed with people not sure which way to move, or whether to walk, run or stay where they were. Some on the ground floor made a successful dash for the doors. Others were too hemmed in to reach them. Some in the galleries made a rush for the stairs, but there were already people on the stairs, who were not sure what was happening, and became little more than punching bags for the would-be escapees. People fell and were trodden under foot in the chaos. A railing on one flight of stairs broke away, propelling some upon the crowd beneath them. Some even jumped from the lower gallery, so terrified were they.

As some made good their escape, people outside the building, seeing this and unaware of what was going on inside, tried to force their way in, making it even harder for those trying to get out. People were pushed. Men and women fell. More were trampled by the feet of those with little idea of what was going on.

Spurgeon was stunned. He could not see clearly all that was happening, as the main escape routes were at the far end of the hall from him. He was at first unaware of the seriousness of the situation. He had heard the shouts, but could not distinguish what had been said. However, he could see that many were trying to leave and he could hear the hubbub of thousands of voices raised in anguish, and he gradually became aware that something was seriously amiss. He called for calm, and some in the congregation returned to their seats. But many others did not and continued in their dash to the crowded exits.

What should he do amidst such disruption? Should he continue the service and hope that by so doing he would bring calm? Or should he abandon it and urge the people to leave the building in an orderly fashion and go home? Spurgeon was unsure how bad things were at the far end of the hall and had no idea what was happening on the staircases.

Then another cry was heard. 'Preach! Preach!'

Spurgeon thought there was a fair degree of sanity in that idea. The people had come to hear him, so perhaps his preaching would bring calm. He announced his text. 'The curse of the Lord is in the house of the wicked; but he blesseth the habitation of the just' (Proverbs 3:33). He began to preach and more returned to their seats, but still there was turmoil at the far end of the hall, in parts of the galleries, and though Spurgeon could not see it, on the stairs.

He preached for a few minutes but then realised that it was hopeless. Loud cries were coming from the injured and many were still trying to push through the crowds to escape from the danger. The tempest would not be calmed. The panic was barely eased. He stopped preaching, dismissed the congregation and collapsed into a chair with his head in his hands.

Doctors in the crowd began to attend to the injured. It was soon clear that some of them were in a serious condition.

Spurgeon was greatly distressed. It had now become obvious to him that the situation was a most serious one. His emotions rose to the surface and the tears began to flood. He walked with the assistance of a couple of church leaders into the adjoining room, and collapsed on the floor. He was helped to his feet.

'What's happened? What's happened?' he cried; his voice breaking as he spoke.

'You can do nothing, Mr Spurgeon. We had better get you home.'

'No! No! Not yet! What happened? Are some hurt? What is being done for them? I must know.'

'Sit down, Mr Spurgeon. Sit down. Calm yourself.' Spurgeon sat, though whether he knew what he was doing was far from clear. He covered his face with his hands and wept.

They made an attempt to answer his questions. 'Someone called out "Fire!" and that caused a panic, I'm afraid. The injured are being cared for. Please don't distress yourself, pastor. We'll try to find out more.'

Gradually, and finally in a more orderly fashion, the hall emptied. The only people who remained were the dozens of injured, their relatives and those trying to help them. Also scattered around were the bodies of those who were beyond help.

Spurgeon did not know how bad it was but he knew enough to realise that there had been a terrible disaster. He shook in anguish at the dreadful situation. He was helped into his carriage and taken home. A servant opened the door and was horrified to see her master in such a distressed condition. He was led into the parlour and helped into a chair. Susanna had been lying down, resting. She had given birth to twins only a month before and she was still unwell. It was some time before she appeared and when she did, she was shocked to see her husband so emotionally distraught. A deacon hastily explained to her what had happened, and she rushed to her husband's side. Charles Spurgeon cried and cried and cried.

Though Spurgeon did not find out until later, seven in that vast congregation had died and 28 others had been taken to hospital with serious injuries. Many more had minor injuries.

There had not been a fire. The building had not been in danger of collapsing. It had all been a sick joke but a joke with disastrous consequences.

The next day the newspapers were full of it. Some were sympathetic. Some were critical. One even suggested that the leaders of the church were so lacking in feeling that a collection had been taken while the injured and dying covered the floor.

With the furore surrounding the disaster and because of the stressed condition of their pastor, the church's leaders encouraged him to move to the country for a week to recover. For the remainder of that week and into the next he was severely distressed.

He later wrote that at that time:

'I refused to be comforted; tears were my meat by day and dreams my terror by night. I was in a strange land and a stranger in it. My Bible, once my daily food, was but a hand to lift the sluices of my woe. Prayer yielded no balm to me. My thoughts, which had been to me a cup of delights, were like pieces of broken glass, the piercing and cutting miseries of my pilgrimage.'

Such was his agony of mind it seemed unlikely that he would recover to preach on the following Sunday. The more pessimistic were even wondering whether he would ever preach again.

About a week after that terrible tragedy he was walking with Susie in a garden in Croydon when a passage of Scripture suddenly flashed into his mind. 'Wherefore God also hath highly exalted him, and given him a name which is above every name; that at the name of Jesus every knee should bow, of things in heaven, and things in earth, and things under the earth; and that every tongue should confess that Jesus Christ is Lord to the glory of God the Father' (Philippians 2:9-11).

This caused him to think, 'If Christ be exalted, let Him do as He pleases with me; my one prayer shall be that I may die to self and live wholly for Him and for His honour.' He turned to Susie and said, 'Dearest wife, how foolish I have been. What does it matter what becomes of me if the Lord shall but be glorified?' He later wrote that at that moment, 'The burning lava of my brain cooled in an instant. My prison door was opened. My spirit mounted to the stars.' He had felt as if he had been 'lying in a ditch to die', but now he recognised anew that 'Christ has won the victory' and he had to rise and get back to the fight.

On the Sunday after the disaster Alexander Fletcher took the services at New Park Street. The following week Spurgeon returned to the New Park Street pulpit. In his prayer he said,

> 'We are assembled here, O Lord, this day, with mingled feelings of joy and sorrow: joy that we meet each other again, and sorrow for those who have suffered bereavements. Thanks to Thy Name! Thanks to Thy Name! Thy servant feared that he should never be able to meet this congregation again; but Thou hast brought him up out of the burning fiery furnace, and not even the smell

of fire has passed upon him. Thou hast, moreover, given Thy servant special renewal of strength, and he desires now to confirm those great promises of free grace which the gospel affords. Thou knowest, O Lord, our feelings of sorrow! We must not open the sluices of our woe; but, O God, comfort those who are lingering in pain and suffering, and cheer those who have been bereaved! Let great blessings rest upon them, the blessings of the covenant of grace, and of this world, too. And now, O Lord, bless Thy people!

'We have loved one another with a pure heart fervently; we have rejoiced in each other's joy, we have wept together in our sorrow. Thou hast welded us together, and made us one in doctrine, one in practice, and one in holy love. Oh, that it may be said of each individual now present with us that he is bound up in the bundle of life! O Lord, we thank Thee even for all the slander, and calumny, and malice, with which Thou hast allowed the enemy to honour us; and we pray Thee to grant that we may never give them any real cause to blaspheme Thy holy Name! We ask this for our Lord Jesus Christ's sake. Amen.'

He then preached on the text that had restored his spirits: 'Wherefore God also hath highly exalted him' (Philippians 2:9). In that sermon he made a brief reference to the tragedy but asked his people to excuse him from saying more about it. For, if he did, he thought that he 'should speedily be forced to be silent'. He then expressed his confidence that 'I shall preach again at that place. God shall give us souls there, and Satan's empire shall tremble more yet.'

Two weeks later he took the brave step of returning to Surrey Gardens. As he gazed out upon the immense assembly he was once more overcome with emotion. It brought back such terrible memories. The next week Spurgeon was again in that pulpit.

This tragic event never left Spurgeon. It hovered over him through the rest of his life and would seem to have been one of the reasons for his poor health after it. But he was now ready to continue his powerful ministry.

The injured and the bereaved were not forgotten. Spurgeon set up a fund to aid them. He and some of the leaders in the church also visited them. An inquest was held some months later into the deaths. It handed down the verdict of accidental death.

CHAPTER 9

THE SURREY GARDENS MINISTRY

'Our harvest is too rich for the barn.' (C H Spurgeon)

The leaders of New Park Street decided to continue to hold services at the Surrey Gardens Music Hall, but in the morning rather than the evening. The evening services were to be at their chapel. The main reason for the change was as fewer people were expected to attend Surrey Gardens in the morning, dangerous overcrowding was less likely. The crowds kept coming, but they were, as expected, smaller and easier to control. Spurgeon continued to preach in that hall for three years. The last service there was held on 11 December 1859.

The congregation was diverse. The poor attended, as did the middle class, and quite a number of the educated and the rich. Some of the leading figures that went to hear Spurgeon included Lord Shaftesbury, Lord John Russell, and other members of the aristocracy, William Gladstone and other politicians, David Livingstone and leading clergy from a variety of denominations. Some even said that Queen Victoria went to hear Spurgeon, though in disguise. While this is probably untrue, that such a claim should be made indicates the status he had acquired.

But it was clear to Spurgeon and the other church leaders that many from outside Christian churches attended. Some sat reading a newspaper until Spurgeon entered the pulpit, which one would not expect from those familiar with Christian worship. While, in one respect, this practice did not please Spurgeon and his deacons, they recognised that this indicated that they were attracting people who needed the Gospel. They were not just ministering to the converted.

Spurgeon was aware of the mixed nature of the Surrey Gardens congregation. He did not find preaching in that environment easy. He later wrote,

'When I began to preach at the Surrey Gardens, I had such a diversified congregation as few men have ever had to address from Sabbath to Sabbath. God alone knows what anxiety I experienced in selecting my subjects and arranging my appeals for such a vast fluctuating assembly. There was a time when my brain was all in a whirl at the very thought of ascending that pulpit, while for all the services among my own people I enjoyed the greatest liberty, with the confidence of one who felt his heart at ease amidst the home-circle of his own family. There was all the difference between preaching in the hall, and in the chapel, that might be expected from the contrast between the neutral ground occupied in the one case and the sacred prestige enjoyed in the other.'

However, the make-up of the Music Hall congregation did change over time, as those who came to see and hear a freak were either converted and stayed, or were untouched by the message and left. Spurgeon sensed the difference, though how much of that was due to his becoming used to addressing that large, mixed assembly, is unclear.

He also adjusted his sermon matter to suit what was, in part, a less biblically aware congregation. While in the services at New Park Street, he delved into deep theological truth; at Surrey Gardens, at least in the early months, he preached more simply. He preached there, he said, 'in plain, homely Saxon that a child could comprehend'.

During this period there was a gradual change in how Spurgeon was perceived by the press and the general population. He was criticised less often and praised more frequently. His abilities, even his preaching style, became more appreciated by those who put pen to paper. Many of the common people loved him from their first hearing, but most of the more prominent citizens took a while to recognise his greatness.

The diarist Charles Greville, a man educated at the famed Eton College, went to hear Spurgeon at the Surrey Gardens in February 1857. He described him as 'remarkable, and undeniably a fine character', with 'a very clear and powerful voice, which was heard throughout the hall'. He had 'wonderful fluency and command of language' and his sermon abounded 'in illustration, and very often of a familiar kind, without anything ridiculous or irreverent'. On this occasion Spurgeon preached for about 45 minutes, and according to Greville, 'to judge by the use of handkerchiefs and audible sobs, with great effect'.

The *Times* newspaper often criticised evangelical Christianity, especially that outside the Church of England. However, it published in one issue a leading article and a lengthy letter praising Spurgeon. The letter gives a clear picture of what it was like at Surrey Gardens. It ran:

'Fancy a congregation of 10,000 souls streaming into the hall, mounting the galleries, humming, buzzing and swarming – a mighty hive of bees, eager to secure at first the best places, and at last any place at all. After waiting half an hour – for if you wish to have a seat, you must be there at least that space of time in advance – Mr Spurgeon ascended the tribune. To the hum and rush and trampling of men succeeded a low, concentrated thrill and murmur of devotion, which seemed to run at once like an electric current through the breath of everyone present.'

Then Spurgeon led the service through, with hymns, scripture readings, prayers and the sermon. The writer of the letter was deeply impressed. The 'power and volume' of Spurgeon's voice, he said, were able to make him heard by 'everyone in that vast assembly'. Spurgeon's 'style', he thought, was 'at times familiar, at times declamatory, but always happy and often eloquent'. He continued that, in his address, Spurgeon waged the battle 'against irreligion, cant, hypocrisy, pride and those secret bosom sins which so easily beset a man in daily life'. The writer was also greatly impressed by Spurgeon's obvious sincerity. He closed by suggesting that the Church of England should invite him to preach at St Paul's Cathedral or Westminster Abbey. No such invitation was ever received.

However, he was invited to speak at the Crystal Palace on 7 October 1857 for the Day of National Humiliation, concerning the 'Indian Mutiny'. That had been a terrible event with atrocities from both sides, and there existed deep feeling in Britain about it.

The Surrey Garden Music Hall was big but the Crystal Palace was bigger. It was estimated that over 20,000 could pack inside the glass-panelled building.

A few days before the first service, Charles visited the Palace to test its acoustics. He knew it would not be easy to project his voice to all in that vast assembly, so he wanted to give it a trial run. When he arrived there were dozens of workmen around the building, preparing it for the service and a handful organising the preparations. He was introduced to the man in charge of the event.

'And where will I be preaching?' he asked.

'Over here, Mr Spurgeon. There'll be a pulpit to give you a little elevation, but it will be quite a task to make yourself heard by everybody.'

'Yes, it will.' Spurgeon was familiar with the building, but he had never considered it as a preaching venue before. 'Over here, you say?'

'Yes, that's right.'

Spurgeon stood on the spot indicated. He paused, gathered himself and then his powerful voice boomed out: 'Behold the Lamb of God, which taketh away the sin of the world' (John 1:29).

Everything stopped. The carpenters ceased hammering, the caterers stopped rattling crockery and cutlery, and the organisers ceased talking. For a few moments there was silence. They all looked at the tiny figure near the front of the hall. Then the noise began again.

When one of the workmen arrived home that night, he pulled a dusty Bible off its shelf, found the text Spurgeon had spoken and read it to himself. His tears began to flow as he recognised that his sin was in part responsible for the death of Jesus, the Lamb of God. Christ became real to him that night.

Conversions abounded at the Surrey Gardens and so did God-ordained incidents. On one occasion, Spurgeon pointed directly to a man in the congregation. It was not that he knew anything about him. Indeed, probably several people in that vicinity thought he was pointing at them. There was nothing unusual in that action for he often did it. The preacher's idea was to strike the message home to each individual.

But then Spurgeon said, 'There is a man sitting there, who is a shoemaker; he keeps his shop open on Sundays. It was open last Sabbath morning, he took ninepence, and there was fourpence profit out of it. His soul is sold to Satan for fourpence!' To Spurgeon, no doubt, that was a general reference. There would have been many in that hall who would break the Sabbath and many there who would sell their soul for money.

A few weeks later a London city missionary was doing his rounds when he came across a shoemaker reading one of Spurgeon's sermons. 'Do you know Mr Spurgeon, then?' the missionary asked.

'Yes,' replied the man. 'I've every reason to know him. I've been to hear him and under his preaching, by God's grace, I have become a new creature in Christ Jesus. Shall I tell you how it happened?'

'Yes! Yes, indeed!' said the excited missioner.

'Well, I went to the Music Hall and took my seat in the middle of the place. Mr Spurgeon looked directly at me as if he knew me. And in his sermon he pointed to me, directly at me,' he said with emphasis.

'And he told the congregation that I was a shoemaker, and that I kept my shop open on Sundays. And I usually did, sir. I shouldn't have minded that, but he also said that I took ninepence the Sunday before, and that there was fourpence profit out of it. And I did take ninepence that day, and fourpence for profit. But how he could know that I couldn't tell. Then it struck me that it was God who had spoken to my soul through him. At first, I was afraid to go again to hear him lest he should tell the people more about me. But I did shut up my shop the next Sunday and on another, and the Lord met with me and saved my soul.'

There was humour too. With Spurgeon it was usually not far away. During his time at the Surrey Gardens 'an unknown censor of great ability used to send' him 'a weekly list of' his 'mispronunciations and other slips of speech'. Yet, Spurgeon's account continued,

'He never signed his name, and that was my only cause of complaint against him, for he left me with a debt which I could not discharge. With genial temper, and an evident desire to benefit me, he marked down most relentlessly everything which he supposed me to have said incorrectly. Concerning some of his criticisms, he was himself in error; but, for the most part, he was right, and his remarks enabled me to perceive many mistakes, and to avoid them in the future. I looked for his weekly memoranda with much interest, and I trust I am all the better for them. If I repeated a sentence which I had used two or three Sundays before, he would write, 'See the same expression in such-and-such a sermon,' mentioning the number and page. He remarked, on one occasion, that I too often quoted the line, 'Nothing in my hand I bring' and he added, 'we are sufficiently informed of the vacuity of your hand.' Possibly, some young men might have been discouraged, if not irritated, by such severe criticisms; but they would have been very foolish, for, in resenting such correction, they would have been throwing away a valuable aid to progress.'

Spurgeon's health was by this time beginning to decline. In his early years he often preached ten or more times a week at his own church and others. With this heavy schedule and the distress of the Surrey Gardens disaster his health went from one problem to another. He had gout, rheumatism and depression, and later, other medical conditions. He was too ill to preach from 10 October to 7 November 1858, so he had an enforced break. But after that, it was back to Surrey Gardens in the morning and New Park Street in the evening.

His last sermon at the Music Hall on 11 December 1859 was taken from Paul's farewell address to the Ephesian elders in Acts chapter 20:26-27: 'Wherefore I take you to record this day, that I am pure from the blood of all men. For I have not shunned to declare unto you all the counsel of God.'

Spurgeon said,

'If any of us would clear our conscience by delivering all the counsel of God, we must take care that we preach, in the first place, the doctrines of the gospel. We ought to declare that grand doctrine of the Father's love towards His people from before all worlds. His sovereign choice of them, His covenant purposes concerning them, and His immutable promises to them, must all be uttered with trumpet tongue.

'Coupled with this, the true evangelist must never fail to set forth the beauties of the person of Christ, the glory of His offices, the completeness of His work, and, above all, the efficacy of His blood. Whatever we omit, this must be in the most forcible manner proclaimed again and again. That is no gospel which has not Christ in it; and the modern idea of preaching *the truth* instead of Christ, is a wicked device of Satan.

'Nor is this all, as there are three Persons in the Godhead, we must be careful that they all have due honour in our ministry. The Holy Spirit's work in regeneration, in sanctification, and in preservation, must be always magnified from our pulpit. Without His power our ministry is a dead letter, and we cannot expect His arm to be made bare unless we honour Him day by day.

'Upon all these matters we are agreed, and I therefore turn to points upon which there is more dispute, and consequently more need of honest avowal, because more temptation to concealment.

'I question whether we have preached all the counsel of God unless predestination, with all its solemnity and sureness, be continually declared; unless election be boldly and nakedly taught as being one of the truths revealed of God. It is the minister's duty, beginning from the fountain-head, to trace all the other streams; dwelling on effectual calling, maintaining justification by faith, insisting upon the certain perseverance of the believer, and delighting to proclaim that gracious covenant in which all these things are contained, and which is sure to all the chosen, blood-bought seed.

'There is a tendency in this age to throw doctrinal truth into the shade. Too many preachers are offended with that stern truth which the Covenanters held, and to which the Puritans testified in the midst of a licentious age. We are told that the times have changed, that we are to modify these old (so-called) Calvinistic doctrines, and bring them down to the tone of the times; that, in fact, they need dilution, that men have become so intelligent that we must pare off the angles of our religion, and make the square into a circle by rounding off the most prominent edges. Any man who does this, so far as my judgment goes, does not declare all the counsel of God.

'The faithful minister must be plain, simple, pointed, with regard to these doctrines. There must be no dispute about whether he believes them or not. He must so preach them that his hearers will know whether he preaches a scheme of free-will, or a covenant of grace; whether he teaches salvation by works, or salvation by the power and grace of God.

'But, beloved, a man might preach all these doctrines to the full, and yet not declare all the counsel of God. It is not enough to preach doctrine; we must preach duty, we must faithfully and firmly insist upon practice. So long as you will preach nothing but bare doctrine, there is a certain class of men, of perverted intellect, who will admire you; but once begin to preach responsibility, to say outright, once for all, that if the sinner perish, it is his own fault, that if any man sinks to hell, his damnation will lie at his own door, and at once there is a cry of "Inconsistency! How can these two things stand together?"

'Even good Christian men are found who cannot endure the whole truth, and who will oppose the servant of the Lord who will not be content with a fragment, but will honestly present the whole gospel of Christ. I say it solemnly, I do not believe that any man is even faithful to his own conscience, who can preach simply the doctrine of Sovereignty, and neglect to insist upon the doctrine of responsibility. I do assuredly believe that every man who sinks into hell shall have himself alone to curse for it.'

There the Surrey Gardens ministry ended. But this sermon clearly demonstrates that if he was reluctant to preach profound doctrine in his early months at the Music Hall, he certainly did so by the close of his ministry there.

CHAPTER 10

THE METROPOLITAN TABERNACLE

Charles Spurgeon was 'so wonderful a man, and yet so simple, with a great child-heart; or rather, so simple because so great, needing no scaffoldings of pompous mannerism to buttress up an uncertain reputation; but universally esteemed, because he cared nought for human opinion, but only for what was upright, open-hearted, and transparent, both in ministry and life. We never knew a public man who had less of self about him, for over and above aught else, his sole ambition seemed to be, "How can I most extol my Lord?"' (Pastor Hugh D Brown, of Dublin).

In 1856 the New Park Street leaders had decided that they must build a new, bigger church and in September a building fund was set up. The fund progressed well but finding a suitable site proved difficult. It needed to be large, accessible to traffic and affordable. The solution came from the quaintly named Worshipful Company of Fishmongers. (The WCF is one of the Livery Companies of the City of London.) In the mid-19th century that company operated a complex with a number of almshouses (small homes for the poor) in Newington. These almshouses had moved to Wandsworth in the early 1850s, so the Company of Fishmongers now had land for sale in Newington, which was the borough next to Southwark. Therefore, if the New Park Street Church was able to buy that land, it would not have to move far.

This site was especially attractive to Spurgeon. Nearly 300 years before a small group of Baptists had been martyred nearby, and it greatly appealed to him to build a Baptist church near where they had died so bravely.

On 13 December 1858, a church meeting was held at New Park Street, at which it was announced that the land had been purchased for £5,000. The funds so far raised covered that, with a surplus of £3,600, which was to go towards the building and other expenses. At that stage the expected cost of building was approximately £16,000, but Spurgeon, knowing that such projects usually cost more than expected, estimated that about £20,000 was needed. This meant that they still needed to raise more than £16,000 and in mid-Victorian England that was a huge sum.

Inevitably, there was criticism about the erecting of this new church, which it was hoped would seat 5,000. Some in the New Park Street congregation felt that they were overstretching themselves. Some newspapers condemned it as too ambitious. But Spurgeon saw it as necessary:

> 'For my own part, I have no such wish for such a large sanctuary; only I cannot bear to see Sabbath after Sabbath as many go away as are able to enter the chapel where we have been accustomed to assemble for worship. It is the will of the people to come in great multitudes to listen to my proclamation of the truths of the gospel. I have not asked them to come. It is of their own free will that they meet with us; and if it is a sin for me to have so many hearers, it is at least an uncommon sin, which many others would like to commit if they could.'

As has been seen, Spurgeon hated debt and refused to fall into it even for building a church. 'We will not go into debt for the house of God,' he said. 'I decline to preach in the place until it is paid for.'

Yet Spurgeon was confident the money would be raised. He said,

'"How are we to get it?" Pray for it. When I thought of the large sum, I said to myself, "It may as well be twenty thousand as ten; for we shall get one amount as readily as the other."' He was confident that they would raise the money, because he knew that he had a praying people and a generous God. In answer to that faith £1,000 was given and promised at that meeting.

But what should the building look like? How should it be designed? The building committee set out some specifications, which were sent to various architects and prizes were offered for the best designs submitted. Over 60 plans were received and eventually the design of William Wilmer Pocock was accepted; modifications to it were suggested and eventually made. Pocock was a Methodist lay preacher and an experienced architect, who designed a number of churches.

The project was then tendered. The lowest tender was £20,000, which was gladly accepted. This was the precise figure Spurgeon had estimated. However, more money would be required for furnishings and fittings.

The foundation stone was laid on 16 August 1859. By January 1860, the building fund was up to nearly £17,000, with £2,000 more by April. The money kept coming in bit by bit, but with rising costs, there was still much more needed.

Then Spurgeon had a providential encounter. He had been visiting a country church when a wealthy business man invited the preacher to join him in his carriage. Spurgeon climbed up and sat beside him. The man introduced himself, then with great energy said, 'You've got to build that big place.'

Spurgeon smiled. 'Yes, we will. We will.'

'Many of your friends feel nervous over the financial situation, you know.'

'Yes, I realise that.'

'What do you think would be needed to finish it? Altogether, I mean! Everything, including the fittings!'

'I think we might need another £20,000.'

The man paused for a moment's thought. 'Alright, I will guarantee you the £20,000.'

Spurgeon's eyes lit up.

'But on one condition,' continued the man, 'that you only use what you need to finish the building with its fittings. After you have met all your commitments you have no claim on whatever is unused of the £20,000. Is that clear?'

'Yes, oh yes,' responded the delighted Spurgeon. 'I am most grateful to you.'

With that they shook hands and Spurgeon climbed down from the carriage, which soon pulled away.

Spurgeon returned to London. In the following months other donations continued to arrive. In the end, little of that man's generous offer was used but it was always a safeguard against the church going into debt.

The building was completed in 1861 and dedicated that March. It had a long sloping ground floor area with two extensive galleries, and was able to accommodate the hoped-for 5,000 people. Below the main worship area was a large lecture hall, which held over 800, and several sizable rooms large enough to accommodate 1,000 Sunday School children. One of the proposed uses of the lecture hall was to accommodate the prayer meetings, which even at New Park Street had hundreds in attendance.

The pulpit was level with the lower gallery and it had plenty of room for Spurgeon to move. Beneath it was the baptistery. Above the pulpit was a strategically placed clock, not that many would have looked at it while Spurgeon was preaching. Clock-watching and sleeping were not common when Spurgeon was in action. In fact, he once said, 'If anyone goes to sleep while I am preaching, don't wake them up; wake me up.'

Through most of the lengthy process of planning and building, the church had continued to meet at Surrey Gardens in the morning and at New Park Street in the evening. That arrangement was far from satisfactory, but it did assure that thousands heard the Gospel and that the church maintained its identity. During that time, Spurgeon said that they had experienced 'many difficulties, but far more providences.'

Now the church, which by this time had more than 1,500 members, had its own extensive and functional premises. And it was free of debt.

The first meeting held in the completed building was a prayer meeting. At 7am on Monday 18 March 1861, more than 1,000 people gathered together for prayer and thanksgiving to God the provider. The next Monday another well-attended meeting for prayer was held at the same hour. That afternoon Spurgeon preached the first sermon in the Tabernacle. His text was 'And daily in the temple, and in every house, they ceased not to teach and preach Jesus Christ' (Acts 5:42). The following weekend was Easter and Spurgeon preached in the Tabernacle twice on Good Friday and twice on Easter Sunday. On Tuesday evening 9 April, the baptistery was used for the first time with Spurgeon baptising about 20 people. Early in June, Spurgeon received 121 into the membership of the Tabernacle. The church was growing at a rapid rate.

Spurgeon's vision was vast. 'It is easy enough for God to double our numbers,' he told his people. What is more 'We shall find ministers raised up and trained and sent forth to carry the sacred fire to other parts of the globe. Japan, China and Hindustan shall have heralds of the cross, who have here had their tongues touched with the Divine flame. Through us the whole earth shall receive benedictions. If God shall bless us, He will make us a blessing to multitudes of others.' His mission clearly did not stop at the boundaries of south London.

While Spurgeon's main concern was with evangelism, his ministry did not end there. In 1862 there was a famine in the north of England that was causing great suffering. One Sunday he preached from Job 30:25: 'Did not I weep for him that was in trouble? Was not my soul grieved for the poor?' He made good the opportunity and appealed for funds to aid those in the famine areas. Nearly £800 was raised.

***

On 15 March 1863 Spurgeon delivered what became his 500th published sermon. Demand for his printed addresses had not declined; it had increased. This widened his ministry considerably for they were read not only in England but in many other lands too.

His text on this occasion was 'Then Samuel took a stone, and set it between Mizpeh and Shen, and called the name of it Ebenezer *[which means "stone of help"]*, saying, "Hitherto hath the Lord helped us"' (1 Samuel 7:12). 'It is certainly a very delightful thing to mark the hand of God in the lives of ancient saints,' he began, and then mentioned a few examples and stated how God had helped them. 'But, beloved,' he continued, 'would it not be even more interesting and profitable for us to remark the hand of God in our own lives.'

He particularly looked at how God had helped him. 'I, your minister,' he said,

> 'Brought by divine grace to preach this morning the five hundredth of my printed sermons, set up my stone of Ebenezer to God. I thank Him, thank Him humbly, but yet most joyfully for all the help and assistance given in studying and preaching the word to these mighty congregations by the voice, and afterwards to so many nations through the press. I set up my pillar in the form of this sermon. My motto this day shall be the same as Samuel's, 'Hitherto, the Lord hath helped me.' And as the stone

of my praise is much too heavy for me to set it upright alone, I ask you, my comrades in the day of battle, my fellow-labourers in the vineyard of Christ, to join with me in expressing gratitude, while together we set up this stone of memorial.'

To the outside observer the work at the Metropolitan Tabernacle must have seemed like a one-man show. Though Spurgeon was the dominant human force, the work emanating from that place of worship relied on hundreds to make it effective, to make it successful. Spurgeon knew that.

He also preached a sermon against baptismal regeneration in 1864, and he was concerned that he would lose some friends because of it. However, he decided to go ahead with printing and distributing it in the usual way. He need not have worried; it quickly sold 100,000 copies, caused the expected stir and then sold more. Spurgeon was not deliberately controversial or confrontational but he believed that sometimes he had to tackle disputed issues even though some would be upset by that. Indeed, a Baptist's stand on baptism was always controversial in that it rejected infant baptism, which many other churches practised. Yet it was not only Baptists who read his sermons.

When Spurgeon was preaching he concentrated directly upon delivering his message. This did not mean he was unaware of what was going on in other parts of the Tabernacle, at least in the pews visible to him. His deacons used to sit on the platform behind him and in the middle of one sermon he suddenly turned to them and whispered, 'Pickpocket! Mrs Sharpe's pew!' He continued preaching without seeming to miss a beat and two of the deacons went to the rear of the church where a policeman was stationed. They advised him of the problem and its location and the constable made his arrest. The majority of the congregation was unaware of what had happened.

Some thought that the man had been taken ill and had been helped out.

To the leaders of the Tabernacle Spurgeon was 'The Guv'ner' (Governor). This displayed two things: first, the deep respect that they held for him as their leader; secondly, the affection they had for him. Spurgeon was in charge, but he was a lovable and admired leader. He, in turn, referred to the deacons by such names as 'Uncle Tom', 'Dear Old Joe', 'Brother William' and 'Father Olney'. When at times Spurgeon's poor health meant that he had to absent himself from the pulpit, Spurgeon asked his deacons, 'Aren't you tired of having a crippled pastor?'

One deacon quickly responded, 'We would sooner have you for one month in the year than anyone else in the world for twelve.'

CHAPTER 11

SPURGEON IN EUROPE

Charles and Susie had spent their honeymoon in Paris but it was not to be the great preacher's last visit to continental Europe. In later years, as his health declined, he usually spent the winter months in southern France for its warmer weather. He also ministered in France and other continental lands in his earlier years.

It was in the summer of 1860 that he took his first significant holiday since his honeymoon. He left London with Susie and two friends early in June and did not return until near the end of July.

They first landed in Antwerp in Belgium. In that city he was horrified by the vast number of statues of Mary he saw scattered around. He said, 'You cannot turn the corner of a street without seeing them.' The sight of them greatly disturbed him. 'Never did I feel my Protestant feelings boiling over so tremendously as in this city of idols.' However, he was more than ready to admit that 'there are some of God's people even in' Roman Catholicism.

They next moved on to Brussels where he 'heard a good sermon in a Romish church'. The church was crowded and Spurgeon had to stand but 'the good priest preached the Lord Jesus with all his might'. The Englishman's knowledge of the French language was good enough to understand much of what the preacher said, and Spurgeon's 'heart kept beating within' him as the man 'told of the beauties of Christ and the preciousness of his blood, and of his power to save the chief of sinners'. While there were 'objectionable sentences' in the sermon, Spurgeon felt he could have gone to the man afterwards and said, 'Brother, you have spoken the truth.'

They then travelled along the River Meuse, the loveliness of which Spurgeon greatly admired. He loved the 'succession of beautiful pearls' he saw, 'threaded on the silver string of that swift-flowing river'. He was not pleased, though, by another sight. As the barges were unloaded, the women carried 'the heavy baskets on their backs' while the men 'were busily engaged in the important occupation of smoking their pipes'. It was no 'joking matter to see poor women compelled to work like slaves, as if they were only made to support their husbands in idleness'.

This caused him to consider the role of women in Britain. 'The fact is,' he said, 'to come to something that may be worth thinking about, employment for women is greatly needed in our country, and the want of it is a very great evil. But it is not so much to be deplored as the barbarity which dooms women to sweep the streets, to till the fields, to carry heavy burdens and to be the drudges of the family. We greatly need that watchmaking, printing, telegraphing, bookselling and other indoor occupations should be more freely open to female industry.'

It was then on to Cologne in Germany. Spurgeon remembered it chiefly for its smell, or more accurately, its smells. One man had said that Cologne had 83 bad odours. Spurgeon thought he had underestimated the number, 'for every yard presented something more terrible than we had ever smelt before'. Bearing in mind that 'our filthy friend the Thames' often had a bad smell, Cologne must have been terrible to have been of special mention.

They then visited Frankfurt, Heidelberg and Baden-Baden. While Spurgeon admired much in Baden, he was highly critical of its casino. He thought it 'to be fraught with the more deadly evils than anything else that could be invented'. He was especially concerned of the effects gambling would have on families. However, a sight opposite the casino cheered him up considerably. There, an agent from the Bible Society was selling Bibles, New Testaments and tracts. Spurgeon spoke to him and bought a New Testament.

Spurgeon was delighted to arrive in Geneva where he met Merle d'Aubigné, the renowned Swiss pastor and author, and César Malan, the hymn writer. But the greatest moment of his visit was preaching from the pulpit that many years previously had been occupied by the great John Calvin. Spurgeon had a high regard for that Reformer and took it as a great honour to preach where Calvin had preached. Yet there was a language problem. Spurgeon had to speak in English, as his French was inadequate for a prolonged discourse, and as he later said, 'I do not think half the people understood me.' Yet he felt that the people joined 'in heart' into the worship of God in spite of the language gap.

There was also a problem with what to wear in the pulpit. Spurgeon usually preached wearing a normal suit but his hosts wanted him to wear clerical robes. This he was reluctant to do. However, 'the request was put to' him so beautifully that he 'could have worn the Pope's tiara if by so doing' he 'could have preached the gospel more freely'. So he wore the robes, though he was not comfortable in the attire.

He fell in love with the Alps. *What extraordinary works of God are to be seen there*, he thought. He heard several avalanches and saw their aftermath but fortunately did not fall foul of any. He was particularly impressed by the Simplon Pass and the man-made road through it. To him it said, 'Man's is little, but over God's greatest works man can find a pathway, and no dangers can confine his ambition.'

Atop one mountain the party visited a hospice run by an order of monks. Spurgeon was impressed by their dedication and hospitality, and was more sympathetic towards them than he otherwise might have been because they were of the Augustinian order, and Augustine was another of his heroes.

When he returned to London he told his people that if they could ever afford it, they should 'go to Switzerland' but only after the Tabernacle was paid for.

***

He made a return visit to Europe in August 1871 with his twin sons, Charles and Thomas. The boys were deeply impressed by their father's knowledge of the local churches, tombs and artistic works. They visited the cathedral while the funeral 'of some great personage' was being conducted. As the Spurgeons witnessed the various practices being followed, Spurgeon senior seethed. There was too much ritual, a lot of which had doubtful pedigree, and it was also 'gloomy'. The funeral was quickly followed by a joyous wedding; the difference between the two ceremonies was most apparent.

The twins were converted by the time they were teenagers and baptised by their father at the same service in September 1874.

It may seem surprising that Thomas and Charles were the only children of Charles and Susannah. It was common in Victorian England for couples to have many children. For example, Queen Victoria had nine and Catherine Booth had eight, and many more examples could be given. The reason why the Spurgeons had no more than two is unknown, but it is known that Susie had a significant medical condition for much of her life and had at least two operations. The doctor who operated on her was James Simpson of Edinburgh, a specialist in gynaecology. It would seem likely that those two matters were linked.

After Simpson operated on Susie, Spurgeon asked him what his fee would be. Simpson replied, 'Well, I suppose it should be a thousand guineas, and when you are the Archbishop of Canterbury I'll expect you to pay it. Until then consider it settled by love.' The lovable Spurgeon attracted that kind of response.

CHAPTER 12

HIS MINISTRY EXPANDS

Spurgeon was first and foremost a preacher and evangelist. Yet his ministry did not end there. The need to tell others about Jesus Christ was his primary motivation but he knew that he could not do it all himself. He also realised that this task did not end with preaching. While hundreds, even thousands, were converted directly through Spurgeon's ministry, many more were converted indirectly.

On the morning of 5 August 1855, early in his ministry, he challenged his congregation to take the Gospel to others. 'I cannot think,' he told them, 'that out of the 1,500 or 2,000 persons now present within the reach of my voice, there are none beside myself who are qualified to preach the gospel.' He went on,

> 'I would like to find scores of preachers among you. "Would God that all the Lord's people were prophets" (Numbers 11:29). There are some here who ought to be prophets, only they are half afraid. Well, we must devise some scheme for getting rid of their bashfulness. I cannot bear to think that while the devil sets all his servants to work, there should be one servant of Jesus Christ asleep. Young man, go home and examine thyself; see what thy capabilities are, and if thou findest that thou hast ability, then try in some humble room to tell to a dozen poor people what they must do to be saved. You need not aspire to become absolutely and solely dependent upon the ministry; but if it should please

God, desire even that high honour. "If a man desire the office of a bishop, he desireth a good work" (1 Timothy 3:1). At any rate, seek in some way to proclaim the gospel of God.'

His congregation took notice of what he had said, for in the mid-1860s there were over 200 people from the Metropolitan Tabernacle engaged in evangelistic work that was encouraged by their pastor. In addition, through the Tabernacle, Spurgeon set up a number of successful and useful ministries, which extended his influence significantly.

The Pastors' College

Probably the most important of these was the Pastors' College. He once said, 'To preach the Gospel myself and to train others to do so is my life's object and aim.'

Spurgeon had never attended a ministerial or theological college. His reading as a child and teenager had been most extensive and his mind absorbed what he read quickly and effectively. He had studied, if you like, at an informal college, and this made a ministerial college unnecessary for him. But not everyone was like Spurgeon. He knew this and realised that potential pastors needed good training.

It was probably late in 1854 or early the following year that Spurgeon began a correspondence with a young man named Thomas Medhurst. Medhurst had first contacted the preacher because he was deeply concerned about his sinfulness, but he could not find Christ the forgiver of sin. Spurgeon recognised his earnestness and replied, giving advice on how he might become a Christian. Medhurst was eventually converted at one of Spurgeon's weeknight services at New Park Street.

Within two months of his conversion, Medhurst was preaching

in the open air. But he was not well educated, which was obvious in his preaching. Some members from New Park Street heard him and complained to Spurgeon. So Spurgeon interviewed him and told him that some were speaking against his preaching. Medhurst responded, 'But I must preach, sir. I must. And I will preach unless you cut me head off.'

That was the kind of response Spurgeon loved. So he arranged for Medhurst to live with another Baptist pastor and to learn from him. Spurgeon also paid his expenses and once a week gave Medhurst further instruction in Christian ministry. The young man developed well and at the end of 1856, became the pastor at Kingston upon Thames Baptist Church in south London.

While he had been tutoring Medhurst, Spurgeon had the idea of educating other young men in the Bible and pastoral ministry, so he began to gather suitable books to establish a library for that purpose. After Medhurst was settled at Kingston, Spurgeon trained another young man by the name of Silverton. Quickly, others also made it known that they wished to be trained for the ministry. This forced Spurgeon's hand. The idea of a training college for Baptist pastors had to become a reality. But where should it be held? What structure should it take? Who should teach in it? Spurgeon was more than ready to lecture on occasions, but he was already overloaded with work, so it was impossible for him to take a major role in it.

Thomas Medhurst now lodged with a well-educated Congregational minister named George Rogers. Spurgeon came to know Rogers and respected him greatly. He was a man with deep theological knowledge and a warm, evangelistic heart. He was, Spurgeon thought, the ideal man to act as principal in a Pastors' College.

But he was not a Baptist.

Whatever doubts Spurgeon had on that score, he quickly washed away. Rogers was ideally suited for the job and he was willing and available, so Spurgeon invited him to become principal of the soon to be formed Pastors' College. Whatever else this shows, it clearly demonstrates that Spurgeon could move outside denominational boundaries. He was a firmly convinced Baptist but he had time and respect for those in other Christian denominations who preached evangelical truth.

So George Rogers became the first principal of the Pastors' College and remained so until 1881. He, a Congregationalist amongst Baptists, said that he felt like a black sheep amongst a washed flock. But he was a more than useful black sheep. He hosted the first intake of eight students in his home and taught them there. After the Metropolitan Tabernacle was built, the students used a schoolroom in its basement. Later, as the number of students grew, separate buildings were constructed near the Tabernacle to house them.

Spurgeon's philosophy for the college was to train 'preachers rather than scholars'. In fact, he only took men who had already shown a gift for preaching. He refused to take men who had, by their own confession, 'failed in everything else' and assumed therefore that they must be called to be preachers. Spurgeon said he had met 'a hundred' like that and he took none of them. Some success in preaching was necessary before admission.

He usually visited the college at the end of each week and lectured in a light and colourful, but informative, vein. He reasoned that after a week of intense study, the last thing the students needed was something heavy. These lectures were published and republished and are still available today.

The lectures were both practical and spiritual. As he said in one of them,

'If I want to preach the gospel, I can only use my own voice; therefore I must train my vocal powers. I can only think with my own brains, and feel with my own heart, and therefore I must educate my intellectual and emotional faculties. I can only weep and agonise for souls in my own renewed nature, therefore must I watchfully maintain the tenderness which was in Christ Jesus. It is not great talents God blesses so much as likeness to Jesus.'

In Spurgeon's lifetime the college produced well over 800 Baptist pastors and missionaries. Pastors from the college went to many places in England, as well as nations as diverse as the USA, Canada, the Falkland Isles, South Africa, North Africa, France, Holland and Haiti.

Amongst these pastors were his own sons, Thomas and Charles. Thomas began his ministry in South Street Baptist Church, Greenwich, and later served for a time in Australia and New Zealand. After a period of pastoral ministry, Charles Junior was placed in charge of the Tabernacle's orphanage.

Requests for pastors came from many places. One request asked for a student who would 'fill the chapel'. Spurgeon replied that he did not have one that large, but he did have one that might fill the pulpit.

Other Baptist Churches

Thomas Medhurst was trained under Spurgeon's influence and became the pastor of the Kingston-upon-Thames Baptist Church. As has been seen, many more followed.

The Baptist Church in England was growing rapidly, particularly in the south-east. And Charles Haddon Spurgeon was the main reason for that growth. By the late-1870s there were well over 40 new churches in the London area that had emerged from or been influenced by his ministry, each with its own mission to the lost.

Amongst these new works were the New Baptist Chapel, Stockwell; Claremont Chapel, Camberwell; East Hill Chapel, Wandsworth; all in the south of London, and Croydon Baptist, just south of London, where James Spurgeon ministered. Spurgeon also aided the newly-formed Highgate Road Baptist Chapel on the fringe of London's north-west.

But Spurgeon did not send his men to any church that requested one. A country church asked for a pastor but offered a ridiculously small wage. Spurgeon responded, 'The only individual I know who could live on such a stipend is the angel Gabriel. He would need neither cash nor clothes. He could come down every Sunday morning and go back at night so I advise you to invite him.' If that sounds unfair, bear in mind that Spurgeon was at the forefront of those who helped smaller churches, but he was not in favour of paying starvation wages to Baptist pastors.

In addition, many individuals with no intentions of becoming pastors were converted through Spurgeon's ministry. Some of these lived nowhere near the Tabernacle, so regular attendance there was impossible. They therefore attended churches near their homes. Others lived near the Tabernacle, but moved to other places for work or other reasons. Many of these joined Baptist churches near their new home, thus boosting the numbers attending these churches.

The Colporteurs

In 1866 Spurgeon wrote an article for *The Sword and the Trowel* about the need for the distribution of good Christian literature. *The Sword and the Trowel* was the Tabernacle's widely-read monthly magazine, which had begun publication that year. Spurgeon's primary concern in that article was to combat the teachings of the High Anglican group, the Tractarians. Spurgeon argued that if the Tractarians could increase their influence through tracts, then so could evangelical Christians.

A member of the Tabernacle congregation soon made a generous offer of funds to launch such a work and a committee was set up to organise it. The work became known as The Metropolitan Tabernacle Colportage Association.

Its aim, rather dramatically put, was 'the increased circulation of religious and healthy literature among all classes, in order to counteract the evil of the vicious publications which abound, and lead to much immorality, crime and neglect of religion'. The literature circulated included Bibles, Christian books, magazines and tracts. Paid colporteurs were employed in strategic areas throughout London, and eventually much further afield, to sell these items, the prices of which ranged from one penny to a shilling. Smaller items, such as tracts, were given away. Some already established shops also became agents of the association and added the books to their existing stock. The British and Foreign Bible Society and the Religious Tract Society supplied some of this literature.

Where those visited were illiterate or too poor to purchase items, the colporteurs would sit down and read stories to them. The colporteurs also engaged in preaching where it was practicable.

One colporteur reported,

'On my visit in October I went as usual amongst the working-men in the granite stone quarry, and I heard a bell ring loudly, and all at once I saw about sixty or seventy men running towards where I was standing. Just what I wanted!

'I found that the bell signified the firing of a shot in the quarry, hence danger. Now they came around the colporteur, listened eagerly to the gospel and bought freely of my good books, nearly emptied my knapsack and nearly filled my pocket with coppers.

'Previous to this I was very weary because of my heavy load of books. How good of the Lord to direct me to the right place at the right time! I came away with a light heart and a light load and offered up my little prayer: "Lord, bless those good books and those few words spoken to the good of the men's precious souls.""

The work grew so rapidly that in 1872 a paid official, W Corden Jones, was appointed to administer it. In 1878 the association had 94 colporteurs, who made over 900,000 visits and sold over £8,000 of books. In 1891 one further colporteur had been added and the sales increased to over £11,000.

Spurgeon's Social Conscience

Amongst the many demands made upon Spurgeon was to take his part on, what one might call, the lecture circuit. One example of this was a lecture he gave for the Young Men's Christian Association (YMCA) in January 1859. The YMCA began in 1844 and one part of its ministry was a series of lectures at Exeter Hall given by a variety of Christian leaders. Speakers had included William Arthur (a Wesleyan Methodist minister), James Hamilton (a Church of Scotland minister), Asa Mahan (the president of America's Oberlin College) and the Honourable W Baptist Noel (an aristocratic minister of the Church of England, who later became a Baptist).

Spurgeon's lecture bore, what for him, was an unusual title, in that it was in Latin: *De Propaganda Fide* (the propagation or spreading of the faith).

In this lecture Spurgeon strongly criticised the opium traffic in China, which had been encouraged by British authorities, and he condemned the ensuing Opium Wars, the second of which was going on as he spoke. In fact, the traffic of opium had become the great scandal of that time in British-Chinese relationships. Opium had been used medicinally both in China and Europe for many years. In the mid-18th century Robert Clive, who established the British Empire in India, recognised the commercial possibilities of that drug. It was being produced in the territory he governed, so he authorised the East India Company to commence exporting it to China.

It is probably true to say that the full social consequences of such trafficking were not realised by anyone at the time. However, as more and more Chinese began to use the drug, the problems became evident. With little other transportation available to get from place to place, some missionaries had used the ships that had also transported opium. In the minds of many Chinese this put the missionaries in the same camp as those in this despised drug trade.

The Chinese had always been cautious about trading with the European powers and they were only willing to conduct such business when they believed it served their best interests. The drug trade obviously did not do that. The resulting disagreement between China and Britain grew to such intensity that war broke out.

British warships sailed into Chinese waters and shelled Chinese ports, and Hong Kong was occupied early in 1841. On 28 August 1842, the Treaty of Nanking was signed, guaranteeing the opening of various major Chinese ports to foreign trade. A second war broke out in the late 1850s. Whatever the wrongs of these Opium Wars, China was now open, not only to commercial trade but also to missionary enterprise: the propagating of the Christian faith.

However, the war was strongly criticised by many in Britain. Dr Thomas Arnold, famous Headmaster of Rugby School, described it as being 'so wicked as to be a national sin of the greatest possible magnitude'. The Christian humanitarian Lord Ashley (later Lord Shaftesbury) called it 'one of the most lawless, unnecessary, and unfair struggles in the record of history'.

In his YMCA lecture in 1859, Charles Spurgeon entered the fray. His subject was spreading the faith, and he dealt with that thoroughly and typically. However, he did not end there. As he drew his address to a conclusion, he began to sail into highly controversial waters. 'I often hear Christian men blessing God for that which I cannot but reckon a curse,' he said. Immediately there was a stir in the audience. 'What is he going to say now?' some wondered. They soon found out.

'They will say, "If there is a war with China, *The bars of iron will be cut in sunder, and the gates of brass shall be opened to the Gospel.*" Whenever England goes to war, many shout, "It will open a way for the Gospel." But I cannot understand how the devil is to make a way for Christ; and what is war but an incarnate fiend, the impersonation of all that is hellish in fallen humanity?

'Let any other nation go to war and it is all well and good for the English to send missionaries to the poor inhabitants of the ravaged countries. But for English canon to make a way for an English missionary is a lie too glaring for me to believe for a moment. I cannot comprehend the Christianity which talks thus of murder and robbery. I blush for my country when I see it committing such terrible crimes in China, for what is the opium traffic but an enormous crime?'

Perhaps here Spurgeon was being a little unfair. One of the war's outcomes was to open the way for missionary enterprise in China but that was not the war's purpose. Rather, its purposes were to trade and colonise. However, that situation presented numerous difficulties for the missionaries who were moving in on the backs of sailors, soldiers and traders.

But not all of Spurgeon's listeners agreed with him. There would have been many in the Exeter Hall that day who believed England could do no wrong and that whatever opened up a country to the preaching of the Gospel must be right. Spurgeon was popular but could his popularity survive such controversy? Yet did that really matter?

Before he finished he also mentioned an incident in which a female missionary gave a tract containing the Ten Commandments to a Mandarin. The Mandarin sent back a polite reply saying that he had never read such good laws but felt that there was more need of them in England and France than in China.

Clearly Spurgeon was not just an evangelist.

The Orphanage

That social conscience was to lead Charles Spurgeon into another venture. Spurgeon was familiar with the work of George Müller of the Brethren and admired him greatly. Müller had established a number of orphanages in the west of England without asking anyone for a penny. When Spurgeon visited Müller's orphanage, he said, 'I never *heard* such a sermon in my life as I *saw* there.'

Spurgeon knew that there was an even greater need for such institutions in London. Poverty was widespread; disease and early death were common. This meant that many children had no parents and often wandered the streets, homeless and uncared for.

In August 1866 he wrote an article in *The Sword and the Trowel* about the children of London and their needs. At about the time that Spurgeon's reference to children appeared in print, he said at a Tabernacle prayer meeting, 'We are a large church and should be doing more for the Lord in this great city. I want us to ask Him to send us some new work; and if we need money to carry it on, let us pray that the means may be sent.' This was a brave declaration for him to make, for though it did not mean that Spurgeon would run the new ministry himself, it would inevitably add to his already extensive cares.

Anne Hillyard was the widow of a wealthy Church of England clergyman. She had a generous heart and wished to give £20,000 to a person or an organisation involved in Christian work with children. She first approached a friend and offered him the money.

'No! No!' he protested. 'I really don't think I am the right person to administer that amount of money. It's too much. You need a public figure. Someone of ability! Someone known to be trustworthy!'

Mrs Hillyard paused for a moment, a blank look on her face. 'But who? But who do you suggest?'

Her friend thought for a moment. A few names went through his mind. Then he said, 'Spurgeon! Spurgeon's the man. The minister at the Metropolitan Tabernacle! Give it to him. He has a good reputation as an honest man. And I'm sure he'll use it wisely.'

So Mrs Hillyard wrote a letter to Spurgeon. She told him that she wished to give him £20,000 for 'the training and education of a few orphan boys'.

When Spurgeon read the letter he at first wondered whether the dear lady had put too many zeroes in the figure. *Perhaps*, he thought, *it should be £200*. But even that was a considerable sum, so he paid her a visit one afternoon, taking William Higgs, a deacon, with him.

Mrs Hillyard warmly invited them in, offered them seats and then arranged for a servant to provide tea. While they were waiting for the refreshments, Spurgeon said, 'We are very grateful, Mrs Hillyard, for your kind offer of £200 towards establishing a home for destitute children.'

'£200! Did I say £200? I said 20,000 and that is what I meant.'

'Ah, well, yes, you did put down £20,000 but we thought it might be a mistake. We thought you might have put in a nought or two, too many.'

'No, Mr Spurgeon, I said 20,000 and I meant 20,000.'

Spurgeon and Higgs looked at each other. Higgs raised his eyebrows. Spurgeon tried to keep his emotions under control but was still cautious.

'Well, Mrs Hillyard, that is very generous of you. But isn't there a relative that you might rather give the money to?'

'No, Mr Spurgeon, there is no one. I have decided to give the money to you for an orphanage.'

The servant came in with the tea and Mrs Hillyard made sure her guests were served. This gave Spurgeon a little more time to think.

'But perhaps you should give it to Mr Müller in Bristol,' he said. 'As you know, he runs a number of orphanages. He looks after hundreds of children.'

'No, Mr Spurgeon. I want to give the money to you for an orphanage for boys. Here in London! I insist upon it.'

Spurgeon did not make a habit of arguing with people willing to give money to his work and he felt that on this occasion he had argued long enough. Clearly that is what the lady wanted to do and it would be foolish, even wrong, to try and persuade her to change her mind. 'Well, Mrs Hillyard, that is indeed generous of you. I will gladly accept the money and use it as you suggest. Thank you so much.'

'I will send you a cheque in the next day or two. More tea?'

Spurgeon declined. Higgs did likewise. The two men took their leave. A few days later the cheque for £20,000 arrived in the mail. More money was received for the home from other sources in small and large donations.

A home for boys was established in 1867. A stained-glass window was set up in one room of the orphanage depicting the all-important meeting between Anne Hillyard, Charles Spurgeon and William Higgs.

It was not until 12 years later that a girls' home was added.

Spurgeon hesitated to commence the girls' work, for by that time his health was in decline and he feared he could not cope with an addition to his labours. But Mrs Hillyard sent £50 towards a home for girls and Spurgeon could not say no to her.

He reported at the time to some friends, 'I have this £50 forced upon me and I cannot get rid of it. Would you have me refuse to use this money for poor fatherless girls? No, your hearts would not so counsel me. Thus, of my own free will, compelled by constraining grace, I accept a further charge and look to see prayer and faith open a new chapter of marvels.'

The homes became known as the Stockwell Orphanage and cared for over 1,500 children in Spurgeon's life time. These children came from a variety of backgrounds and places, though most were from the London region. It did not just cater for children from Baptist families but also for those from a host of other denominations and none. They were accepted on the basis of their need.

Mrs Hillyard was a lifelong supporter of the homes. When she died in 1880, her last words were, 'My boys! My boys!'

Other Ministries

Other ministries included the Book Fund and the Pastors' Aid Society, which were both organised by Susie Spurgeon. Many Baptist pastors of that time were underpaid and struggled to get by, often unable to buy books to aid their ministry.

Just before the publication of the first volume of *Lectures to my Students*, Spurgeon gave his wife a proof copy of it to read. A few days later, he asked her, 'Susie, how do you like *Lectures to my Students*?'

Susie smiled with enthusiasm. 'I wish I could place a copy in the hands of every minister in England.'

Charles thought for a moment, then said, 'Then why not do it?'

Susie responded to the challenge. She had been saving for a while for a worthwhile project, and by this time, had sufficient money for about 100 copies of the book. In a later issue of *The Sword and the Trowel*, they inserted a notice advising pastors that there were 100 free copies of the *Lectures* for those who wished to have one. The response was quick and dramatic. The Spurgeons received nearly 200 requests for the book. However, they lacked the funds to supply the extra copies, so in the following edition of *The Sword and the Trowel*, a scheme was advertised to raise money to pay for books for poor pastors.

Thus, the Book Fund began. The first donation received was an anonymous gift of five shillings worth of stamps. Susie received that gift 'with glad satisfaction'. Years later, she reflected that 'The mustard seed of my faith grew forthwith into "a great tree" and sweet birds of hope and expectation sat singing in the branches.'

In the 15 years that followed, the Book Fund sent out over 120,000 books by Spurgeon and other authors to as many as 6,000 poor pastors of a variety of denominations, not just Baptists. The Pastors' Aid Society developed as an extension of this book ministry and helped those pastors in grave financial difficulties.

In addition, there were the Ordinance Poor Fund, which raised money for the poor, and the Ladies' Benevolent Society, which made and supplied clothes for the underprivileged.

***

On 15 November 1865, the *London Noncomformist* published a survey of the total attendances in the different Protestant denominations in London at all Sunday services, alongside a comparison with 14 years before. The results were:

DENOMINATION	1851 SITTINGS	1865 SITTINGS
Church of England	409,834	512,067
Congregationalists	100,436	130,611
Baptists	54,234	87,559
Wesleyans	44,162	52,454
United Methodist Free Churches	4,858	13,422
Methodist New Connection	984	6,667
Primitive Methodists	3,380	9,230
Church of Scotland	3,886	5,116
English Presbyterians	10,065	12,952
United Presbyterians	4,280	4,860

All the named denominations showed an increase, though the degree of those increases varied considerably. In one respect these improved attendances were no surprise, as there had been a 28-29% increase in the London population during that period. However, the overall increase in church attendances was over 31%, so a little above the rise in the population. There had also been a revival in the British Isles in the late 1850s, which would have been another reason for the improved situation, though this had not impacted London as much as some other places, such as Ireland, Wales and Scotland.

The biggest improvements in this survey were in the Methodist and Baptist denominations. But which increased the most? The dramatic changes in the different Wesleyan/Methodist denominations in this period were caused by many leaving the Wesleyan Methodists and joining other Methodist churches, most notably what became the

United Methodist Free Churches. It is therefore probably best to take the four Methodist groups collectively before comparing them with the Baptists. In 1851 the Methodist total came to 53,384. By 1865 this had been raised to 81,773, an increase of 28,389 or 53%. In that same period the London Baptists showed an increase of 33,325, or 62%. That the Baptists should show the largest increase of the denominations in London was mainly due to the ministry of Charles Haddon Spurgeon. And, as has been seen, Spurgeon's influence extended well beyond London.

In fact, Baptist growth in London and beyond did not end there. In the following 13 years the net increase in membership of British Baptist churches was over 30,000.

CHAPTER 13

SPURGEON AS A PREACHER

'Every now and then someone takes the world by storm… That is the type of man whose influence lives on, and whose figure becomes historical. If we mistake not, Mr Spurgeon belongs to this small class of persons whose career seems independent of circumstances just as their genius is independent of training' (*The Record*, 5 February 1892).

There can be little doubt that Charles Spurgeon was a genius of communication and he would have been a success in any age. But how did he become so?

No one knows how Shakespeare, with perhaps a limited education, could have penned his great works. Some even doubt he did. But he was able to do that because he had an inbuilt gift for language. Mozart was a musical genius. While it is true that he was surrounded by music from his earliest moments, the remarkable talents he displayed as a young child demonstrated an amazing natural gift beyond what he could have learned from others. Each of these men was a genius in a certain field. And as *The Record* said, for a tiny number 'genius is independent of training'.

Spurgeon was like that. But his genius was in communication. He certainly had training in Gospel communication in the homes and churches of his parents and grandparents, but his natural ability went far beyond what he had learnt in those places.

A lot of what he did seemed instinctive. He knew the Bible, he knew theology and he knew church history. But he also knew how to make them sound exciting, relevant and meaningful. He had a powerful and effective voice. He was able to string words together in an understandable and interesting way. He was able to present complex theological ideas simply. He knew how to illustrate graphically in ways which drew his listeners in and helped them understand what he was saying. He used humour and pathos. He touched the mind and the heart.

True, there was a divine dimension in his ministry. God's Holy Spirit brought the harvest, as Spurgeon knew well. He once said, 'I hope I have never preached without an entire dependence on the Holy Ghost.' But he had a natural gift, a God-given talent for being able to place all these pieces together, and that made him a great communicator and a great preacher. It is no exaggeration to call him a genius.

Many considered him the 19th century equivalent of the great George Whitefield, who had taken Britain and America by storm a hundred years before. Yet comparing the two without hearing either would be impossible. Even the best of their written sermons would not communicate the power evident in their original proclamation, so if the sermons of one read better than those of the other it means just that and nothing more.

Both Whitefield and Spurgeon injected great animation and colour into their preaching. Both had powerful voices. But they did not just preach with their voices; their whole bodies, their whole beings were involved in the act. Both preached primarily with the purpose of bringing men and women to Christ. Both attracted great crowds. Both were Calvinists and were not ashamed to let that be known. Both were godly men.

Spurgeon, though, may have been a little more homely in his

language than Whitefield, who had been to Oxford University. He illustrated his sermons with experiences and language that most could understand and apply. And he was, without question, the best preacher of his age.

However, he did not preach to please others, just simply with the aim of attracting people to hear him. He once said, 'I am aware that my preaching repels many; that I cannot help. If, for instance, a man does not believe in the inspiration of the Bible, he may come and hear me once; and if he comes no more, that is his responsibility and not mine. My doctrine has no attraction for that man; but I cannot change my doctrine to suit him.'

It is perhaps surprising that Spurgeon did not adopt the practice of preaching through a book of the Bible in a series of sermons, as many other leading preachers had done, including many of the puritans he loved. He said he was unable to do this. Instead, he picked a verse or verses that had been burning in his mind, prepared his message on Saturday evening and preached on that passage the next day. This meant there was not usually any connection between Spurgeon's sermons week-by-week.

He did not always find the preparing and preaching of sermons easy. Preparing his sermons on Saturday evening generally worked well, as the subject was still fresh in his mind when he preached the next day. Yet one Saturday, it did not go so well. He had his text but was unable to harness his thoughts so that he could develop the message. It looked as though he was going to have a late and stressful night with no certainty of a good result.

Susie was aware of the problem and she had a solution. 'My dear husband, why don't you go to bed now, sleep on it and get up early to finalise your preparation? What won't come together now, may well do so after a night's rest.'

Spurgeon considered the idea but was not enthusiastic about it.

Susie added, 'I promise to make sure that you wake up extra early, so you'll have plenty of time to prepare.'

Spurgeon's mood changed. 'Yes, right! We'll do that.' So saying, he went to bed.

During the night Susie woke up, only to find Charles speaking in his sleep. She listened, as any wife would, and realised that he was expounding the text he'd found so difficult the evening before. She had no pen and paper to hand, so she prayed and made a determined effort to remember all that Charles said. When he had finished talking she went over the points in her mind carefully, then went to sleep.

In the morning both Charles and Susie slept late. When Charles finally woke up he was agitated. The hour of the morning service was drawing close and he had no sermon to preach. What could he do?

'Why did you let me sleep so late?' he asked Susie, accusingly. He was clearly stressed.

Susie was madly scribbling something on a piece of paper. 'You have time. You have plenty of time.'

'What do you mean?' he interrupted. 'I've hardly any time at all. What am I to do?' He paced around in agitation.

'But listen, my dear,' she said. 'Last night you talked in your sleep and what you said was an exposition of the text you had trouble with last night.'

Charles stopped and stared at his wife. 'What do you mean?'

'Look!' she said, showing him the paper. 'This is what you said in your sleep. Or at least, as well as I can remember it.'

Charles took the sheet of paper and peered at it. 'That's it! That's it!' His face, his whole body was animated with delight. 'That's what the text means. That's wonderful. That's wonderful. Isn't our God great, Susie? Praise our God for His goodness!'

'Yes,' she said. 'Praise His Name!'

He rushed to her side, hugged her, then strode to his desk and examined Susie's notes and proceeded to elaborate on them. Well before the time of the service he was ready. He went, he preached and the congregation was not disappointed.

What doctrines did he preach in his ministry? He was, as we have seen, a genuine Calvinist, believing in God's predestination of only some to salvation. In fact, he 'believed in the five great points commonly known as Calvinistic'. These points are total depravity, unconditional election, limited atonement, irresistible grace and the perseverance of the saints. These he taught, these his church adopted. Spurgeon once said, 'The doctrine which I preach is that of the Puritans; it is the doctrine of Calvin, the doctrine of Augustine, the doctrine of Paul, the doctrine of the Holy Ghost.'

The major distinction between Calvinism and Arminianism was that Calvinism held that God elected some to salvation purely out of His sovereign choice, while Arminianism argued that God elected those whom he foreknew would believe the Gospel. Hyper-Calvinism was similar to Calvinism but it so strongly emphasised God's electing some to salvation and not others that it seemed to make evangelism unnecessary, even wrong.

New Park Street Church had, in fact, been traditionally Calvinistic. Spurgeon and his church belonged to the Particular Baptist denomination, that is, the Calvinistic Baptists. Though those Baptist churches formed a denomination each local church was theoretically independent and able to plot its own course.

Yet there was more to Spurgeon's beliefs than those five points. He had a traditional belief in the authority of Scripture as the Word of God, which came especially to the forefront in his final years. He taught the full divinity and humanity of the Lord Jesus Christ. He believed there was one God, though in three persons. And as has been seen, he also believed and taught that baptism should be administered to believers only. His beliefs were consistent with the Westminster Confession of the 17th Century, though with that Baptist twist. In fact, he republished a Baptist version of that confession for the people of his day.

His preaching produced remarkable results, both in the number and the quality of the converts made through his preaching. As he said,

> 'I thank God that I have not had to labour in vain, or to spend my strength for nought. God has given me a long period of happy and successful service, for which, with all my heart, I praise and magnify His holy Name. There has been a greater increase sometimes, or a little diminution now and then; but, for the most part, the unbroken stream of blessing has run on at much the same rate all the while. It has ever been my desire, not to "compass sea and land to make proselytes" from other denominations; but to gather into our ranks those who have not been previously connected with any body of believers, or, indeed, who have attended any house of prayer.

> 'Of course, many persons have joined us from other communities, when it has seemed to them a wise and right step. But I should reckon it to be a burning disgrace if it could be truthfully said, "The large church under that man's Pastoral care is composed of members whom he has stolen away from other Christian churches." But I value beyond all price the godless and the careless, who have been brought out from the world into communion with Christ. These are true prizes.'

Yet it was not through preaching alone that converts were won. He often met with and counselled those who were troubled about their spiritual condition and those just converted. In his words:

'From the very early days of my ministry in London, the Lord gave such an abundant blessing upon the proclamation of His truth that, whenever I was able to appoint a time for seeing converts and enquirers, it was seldom, if ever, that I waited in vain; and, usually, so many came that I was quite overwhelmed with gratitude and thanksgiving to God.

'On one occasion, I had a very singular experience, which enabled me to realise the meaning of our Lord's answer to His disciples' question at the well of Sychar, '"Hath any man brought Him ought to eat?" Jesus saith unto them, "My meat is to do the will of Him that sent Me, and to finish His work"' (John 4:33-34).

'Leaving home early in the morning, I went to the chapel and sat there all day long seeing those who had been brought to Christ through the preaching of the word. Their stories were so interesting to me that the hours flew by without my noticing how fast they were going. I may have seen some 30 or more persons during the day, one after the other; and I was so delighted with the tales of mercy they had to tell me, and the wonders of grace God had wrought in them, that I did not know anything about how the time passed.

'At seven o'clock, we had our prayer-meeting; I went in and prayed with the brethren. After that came the church-meeting. A little before ten o'clock, I felt faint, and I began to think at what hour I had had my dinner, and I then for the first time remembered that I had not had any. I never thought of it, I never even felt hungry, because God had made me so glad and so satisfied with the Divine manna, the Heavenly food of success in winning souls.'

One of the aspects that made Spurgeon so easy to listen to (or read) was that he had the wonderful knack of conveying much meaning in few words. His pithy sayings grabbed the minds of his listeners and made them think.

For example, he said, 'It is no use talking about "the higher life" on Sundays, and then live the lower life on weekdays'; and 'I delight not in the religion which needs or creates a hot head. Give me the godliness which flourishes upon Calvary rather than upon Vesuvius.' It was not that Spurgeon desired or advocated a powerless and dull Christianity, for he was a passionate and Spirit-filled man, but it was that he knew the shouting and hot air some preachers engaged in produced converts full of wind but not the Spirit of God.

Amongst his other sayings were, 'True belief and true repentance are twins; it would be idle to attempt to say which comes first'; 'Do not number your fishes before they are broiled, or count your converts before you have tested and tried them'; 'Revivals, if they are genuine, do not always come the moment we whistle for them'; 'He is no fool who can talk to children'; and 'We all need a religion which can live either in a wilderness or in a crowd.'

One may agree or disagree with any of these statements but they each required the listener to make a response. In fact, Spurgeon's preaching and writing was always geared to encourage a response from his listeners and readers. He did not talk or write just for the sake of pretty words, beautifully expressed.

CHAPTER 14

MORE AT THE TABERNACLE

'Over the Thames to Charlie's' (the cry of a bus conductor, due to cross London Bridge from the north).

What was it like to attend a service at the Tabernacle when Spurgeon was preaching? The following colourful account, which, if not particularly spiritual, is highly descriptive, gives a vivid answer to that question. The unknown writer and his friends knew that getting into the Tabernacle would not be easy because of the large crowds, so they arrived:

'… rather more than half an hour before the stated time of service. A few people were passing the gates with us, but as yet there was no indication of "the crush". Congratulating ourselves on being thus beforehand, we pushed boldly forward, with a view to enter the building by one of its fifteen doors, when there confronted us no less than three scandalised individuals, whose faces wore every expression of horror and indignation. "You cannot get in without a ticket," was the hopeless announcement.

'"Tickets!" we exclaimed. "We have none."

'"Then take your place on the steps," was the chilling rejoinder. "The general public is admitted at five minutes to eleven."

'It was bad enough to have our zeal thus damped at the outset, but to be reminded that we were nothing better than a portion of "the general public" was a hard blow. We did not, however, like to forego the advantage due to our punctuality without an effort. If this had been a concert or a theatre, a piece of silver would doubtless have gained us admission. But the janitors of a place of worship, we considered, were surely not "tippable" subjects.

'While we were rather in a dilemma, a fourth individual came up with a packet of small envelopes in his hand. "I can give you a ticket," he said, "if you wish to go in."

'We were ready to fling our arms round his neck as we gasped "How much?"

'"We make no charge," replied he with the envelopes, handing us one. "But you can put what you like in this towards the support of the Tabernacle, and drop it in yonder box!"

'This, then, was the incantation, the "open sesame" we had been seeking. Seizing the welcome envelope, we retired to a corner, and followed the direction given us. After which, with a proud sense of being rather better than one of the general public, we marched triumphantly forward, inwardly reflecting that whatever the fervour of the spirit animating the authorities of the Metropolitan Tabernacle, their diligence in business was exemplary.

'At ten minutes to eleven we find ourselves in the longed-for pew. There is a buzz of conversation, which is at first quite alarming. "Is this a place of worship or a concert hall?" one mentally inquires. People talk in unabated voices and even laugh, and one of the old ladies in one pew waves her umbrella affectionately to her crony in another. It doesn't seem very reverential, but we put it down to the disturbing effect of a great number of people.

'But all are not here yet. The clock crawls on to five minutes to eleven, and we think of "the general public" outside. A glance shows that there are still a fair number of empty places for them. Then the aisles for the moment resemble the platform of a railway station on an excursion day, at least as far as the eagerness of the candidates for the seats goes. The noise, happily for our reputation as a body of worshippers, is not quite so great. And now every seat is full. The flaps along the aisles are let down and occupied, the gangways in the galleries are packed, the back pews up in the ceiling are tenanted, and we know that at last we are here assembled.

'But how can any one voice make itself heard here, above this hubbub of shuffling and talking and laughing? We are within twenty yards of the platform, and even yet have our misgivings about hearing; and what of those poor "general publicans" away there as far as one can hurl a ball?

'It is eleven o'clock. The door at the back of the platform opens, and a stout, plain man, with a familiar face, advances haltingly to the table, followed by some dozen deacons, who proceed to occupy the stalls immediately behind the pastor's seat.

'Mr Spurgeon said, "Now let us pray," and in an instant there fell a hush over that entire company which, had we not witnessed it, we could scarcely have imagined possible. The first sentence of

Mr Spurgeon's prayer was delivered in absolute silence; and we had no difficulty in setting at peace, once for all, our misgivings as to the possibility of hearing. Dropping coughs presently broke the stillness of the congregation, which sometimes conspired to make an absolute tumult; but from first to last Mr Spurgeon's voice rose superior to all, nay, even seemed to gain power from these very oppositions.

'He read through the opening hymn without strain or effort, and in a voice which must have penetrated to every corner of the building, while a tardy batch of the general public was thronging the aisles and bustling into seats. Mr Spurgeon, we understand, has on more than one occasion said that he can whisper so as to be heard in every part of the Tabernacle, and that he can shout so as to be heard nowhere. In this art lies the secret of his mechanical power as a speaker. It is not by stentorian exertion, but by well-regulated modulation and studied articulation, that he succeeds as he does in bringing all within the compass of his voice. The process is exhausting neither to his audience nor (it would seem) to the speaker.

'To anyone who has not been in a similar scene, a hymn sung by a full congregation at the Metropolitan Tabernacle has a thrilling effect. It is no ordinary thing to see four and a half thousand people rise simultaneously to their feet, still less to hear them sing. For a moment during the giving out of the hymn it occurred to us to look wildly round for the organ, which surely must be the only instrument which could lead all those voices. There is none, and we are sensible of a pang of hurried misgiving as we nerve ourselves to the endurance of all the excruciating torments of an ill-regulated psalmody. A gentleman steps forward to Mr Spurgeon's side as the last verse is being read, and at once raises a familiar tune.

'What is our delight when not only is the tune taken up in all its harmonies, but with perfect time and expression. The slight waving of the precentor's book regulates that huge chorus, as a tap will regulate an engine. The thing is simply wonderful. We feel that tight sensation of the scalp and that quiver down the spine which nothing but the combination of emotion and excitement can produce. We are scarcely able for a while to add our voices to that huge sea of melody which rises and falls and surges and floods the place. If Mr Spurgeon's powers of voice are remarkable, those of his precentor are, to our thinking, marvellous. His voice can be heard above all the others, he holds his own, and is not to be run away with, and in the closing hymn he is as unflagging as in the first.

'"Now, quicker," cries Mr Spurgeon, as we reach the last verse, and it is wonderful to notice the access of spirit which this produced. We sit down, deeply impressed. After all, what instrument or orchestra of instruments can equal in effect the concert of the human voice, especially in psalmody?

'The reading of Scripture followed, accompanied by a shrewd, earnest running commentary, which, though sometimes lengthy, never became wearisome. Mr. Spurgeon is not one of those who believe that Holy Scripture is its own expounder, and certainly in carrying out this view he manages to present the lesson selected in a good deal less disconnected manner than many who, with less ability, attempt a similar experiment.

'Another hymn, chanted, followed, and then a prayer. Mr Spurgeon's prayers are peculiar, their chief characteristic being boldness (to judge by the specimen we heard.) We do not mean to insinuate that he rants, or becomes vulgarly familiar in his addresses to the Deity. But he wastes no words in studied ornament, his petitions are as downright as fervent, and his language is unconventional.

'"This is Thy promise, O Lord," he exclaims towards the close of this prayer, "and Thou mayst not run back from it." We have rarely heard this style of address adopted more freely than by Mr Spurgeon, and we must confess that it does not exactly accord with our prejudices. Still we may safely say the earnestness of his prayer went far to atone for what struck us as the minor defects of language, which, after all, may have been the reverse of defects to the uncritical portion of our fellow-worshippers.

'The most remarkable part of the whole service, however, was the sermon. And here we may as well observe at once, that anyone who goes to the Metropolitan Tabernacle expecting to be entertained by the eccentricities of the preacher is doomed to absolute disappointment.

'We could not help admiring his choice of words. It is pleasant to hear once more half an hour of wholesome Saxon all aglow with earnestness and sparkling with homely wit. You yield yourself irresistibly to its fascination, and cannot help feeling that after all this is better stuff than most of the fine talking and Latin quotations and elaborate periods heard elsewhere.

'Mr Spurgeon told a story in the course of his sermon. It was an extremely simple one about a simple subject, but the effect was remarkable. The coughing gradually died away, or became very deeply smothered, and a complete silence fell on the audience. With masterly skill the speaker worked up the narrative, omitting nothing that could give it power, and admitting nothing that would weaken it. You saw the whole scene before you; you heard the voice of those who spoke; you shuddered at the catastrophe; you sighed when all was over. "And so it is with us," said the preacher, and not another word was necessary to apply the moral.

'While the sermon was going on, we could not resist the impulse to look round and see how our old ladies were enjoying it. It did one good to see one nodding her approval of each sentence, and sometimes lifting her hand to her tell-tale eyes. Another two sat close together, and we are certain that their ribs must have ached by the time it was all over from the amount of mutual nudging that went on. Indeed as we looked round galleries and basement, and saw that sea of attentive faces, we felt reproved for our own inattention, and gave over taking observation, to listen.

'Punctually to the time (and nothing can exceed the punctuality of everything connected with the Tabernacle) Mr Spurgeon closed his Bible, and with it his address. As if relieved from a spell, the congregation coughed and fidgeted and stretched itself to such an extent that, for the first time that morning, the preacher's voice seemed at fault. But the concluding hymn gave ample opportunity for throwing off the pent-up energies of his listeners, and the final prayer was, like the first, pronounced amid a tense silence.'

Spurgeon spoke in the language that people understood and

recounted experiences that all could relate to. His illustrations were picturesque and colourful, and at times a little quaint, though that suited the era in which he lived. He was also brilliant at relating everyday things to spiritual realities. Yet he was deeply theological. His sermons were not light and fluffy. They were profound and thought-provoking, and at the same time, they were energetically evangelistic. His main aim was to win souls to Christ but he also believed that that was only the beginning. Christians also had to be taught the faith. They had to be grounded in solid doctrine.

On one occasion as a boy, he'd been sent by his mother to buy some tea, mustard and rice. On his way home he saw a pack of hounds on the hunt and he did his best to follow them over hedge and ditch. By the time he gave up the chase, the tea, mustard and rice had 'amalgamated into one awful mess'. His mother was not pleased. He applied this lesson to his preaching. He always sought to pack his 'subjects in good stout parcels, bound round with the thread' of his discourse. As Spurgeon said, 'People will not drink mustardy tea, nor will they enjoy muddled up sermons.' Spurgeon's sermons were always clear. That is one of the reasons why so many heard him gladly.

Charles Spurgeon was not just a great preacher. He was also a great motivator. The members of his congregation did not just come to hear mighty words eloquently spoken, they came and were inspired to serve God. His church was a church of doers, not pew-sitters. He did not leave his listeners impressed by the speaker but indifferent to the message. He struck the message home and it was endorsed by the Holy Spirit, and the people were inspired to action. He was a great evangelist and he encouraged others to be evangelists too.

In fact, Spurgeon believed in training his people in evangelism. He knew it was impossible for him to reach everyone, even though he had already reached many. Regular members of his congregation were taught to look out for strangers in the Tabernacle, to speak to them and, if possible, enquire as to their spiritual condition. In addition, the members of his church were employed in offices, shops and other places of work during the week that Spurgeon could not visit. It was these church members who took the Gospel to the people employed in those places.

Yet Spurgeon did not favour, nor did he encourage, a quick, decision type of evangelism. The process leading to his own conversion had been long and difficult as he laboured under conviction of sin for many months. While he did not expect everybody to have the same experience, he did believe that the Holy Spirit must make people aware they were sinners before they could believe in Jesus Christ, the Saviour from sin. Spurgeon believed that people needed to be 'wounded', that is, be made aware of their sin and its seriousness before they could be 'healed' in Christ.

They also needed to know about Christ and His message before they could believe in Him. The evangelist's first task then, was to instruct 'a man that he may know the truth of God', and that instruction should be in-depth and doctrinal: not teaching that only touches the surface. In his book *The Soul Winner*, he said, 'Some of the most glaring sinners known to me were once members of a church and were, as I believe, led to make a profession by undue pressure, well-meant but ill-judged.'

To those who sought to win others to Christ he gave the advice, 'see that you live the gospel' and part of that was to have about them an 'evident sincerity' and an 'evident love' for those to whom they were ministering. They also needed to remember that 'a soul-winner can do nothing without God'. It is God who saves men and women, not human agents, though God does use people in the task.

In January 1868 James Spurgeon, the brother of Charles, was inducted as the assistant pastor at the Metropolitan Tabernacle. The scope of the work at the Tabernacle had become much too large for one pastor, even with an efficient team of elders and deacons to rely on and with others heading up other branches of the work, such as the Preachers' College and the Orphanage. James was an experienced pastor, having previously had successful pastorates in Southampton and London. He was a good preacher and often substituted for Charles when he was sick or touring. James was also a skilled administrator, so he was able to relieve his brother of some of the business side of church life.

One Sunday in the 1870s, Charles preached on Matthew 17:5: 'Hear you Him'.

'When our Lord Jesus Christ was transfigured,' he began...

'There came a voice from the bright, overshadowing cloud, which said, "This is my beloved Son, in whom I am well pleased. Hear you Him." It was the voice of the Father concerning the Son – a testimony to His person, a notification of His office, an announcement of His authority to teach and to legislate. You can understand how imperative it was then for those who heard it to heed Him.'

The effect these few words had upon his listeners was dramatic. There was a deep silence pervading the whole vast assembly. Every face seemed to gaze at the preacher awaiting his next words.

'But now He is gone up from us,' Spurgeon said with emphasis. He paused for a moment then continued,

'He has entered into His excellent glory. He no more teaches in our streets, yet still, as though present with us, He speaks to us. In the written word His sayings are handed down to us infallibly. Often times when the Holy Spirit rests upon God's servants they become as the voice of Christ to us, and when the same blessed

Spirit, as the Comforter, brings to our remembrance the things of Christ, does it not seem as though Jesus, Himself, spoke to our souls? Still does the Father say to us concerning His well-beloved Son, "Hear you him."

'These three little words may give rise to four short questions: Why? What? How? When?

'So why should we hear Him? It might serve for a sufficient answer to that question, had we no other reply, because God Himself commands us! This injunction comes from the Father: "Hear you Him."

'Over and over again we are enjoined to listen to the voice of Christ. Every messenger from God ought to have our respectful attention; how much more the greatest of all messengers – the Messenger of the Covenant, the Messiah, the Sent One? Did not Jehovah Himself say, "This is my Son"? Appointed, anointed, commissioned of the Father to speak to us, to confer with us, to make known among us the mind and will of our great and gracious Sovereign, it becomes treason and blasphemy of the highest order for us to refuse to heed His presence or to listen to His words.

'Why hear Him? Does not our Lord Jesus Christ deserve to be heard? He is peerless among the princes of heaven, very God of very God. And he is immaculate among the children of men. Is he not man of the substance of His mother? Here is a double claim upon our attention: divine and human. He speaks as never man spoke, clothing the highest oracles in the most familiar parables. And will you not hear what this God-Man has to say? Is He not perfect in wisdom, pure in motive and undeviating in truthfulness? If we should not listen to such a one as Jesus of Nazareth – the gentle and meek and lowly, yet the truthful, the honest and the brave – to whom will we ever lend an attentive ear?

'Why will you not hear Him when the message He has come to communicate concerns yourselves, your present and future welfare? The tidings He brings are laden with ten thousand blessings for us, if we will incline our ears and listen to them.'

Once more he paused. Silence reigned, except for a few stifled coughs. Then, once more, his great voice sounded forth: 'You who profess to be His disciples hear Him. If Peter is our master, let us call him so. If Calvin is our master, let us call him so. And if Wesley is our master, let us call him so. But if we are disciples of Jesus then let us follow Jesus. And hear you Him! Prove yourselves to be truly his disciples by listening to Him.' Spurgeon sounded out that final word with great force and it echoed around the vast building.

He continued,

'To the rest – I am grieved at heart that I should have to speak of the rest, but we know there is such a remnant here – to those who are not His disciples, you must hear Him in the Day of Grace, or else you shall hear him in the Day of Judgement and perish forever. Do you refuse to hear Christ? There are no tidings of mercy to be heard elsewhere. O sinners hear the Saviour's voice. O wanderers hear the Shepherd's voice. O you that are dying hear the Physician's voice. They that hear Him shall live. Do you hear Him?'

Once more Spurgeon's voice rose in volume and passion as he uttered that last sentence. But he was far from finished.

'What then are we to hear? There is much to hear concerning the person of Christ, the actions of Christ, the sufferings of Christ and the offices of Christ, but the fullness of all revelation is embodied in Him. Greater than the greatest sermon that was ever preached in the world is the Word made flesh. Would you know God, you must know Christ. In the character of Jesus, the character of God is reflected with divine purity. The invisible God is in Him, made visible to men as far as the sense of faith can behold Him.

'Listen to His voice. He is the wisdom of God and the power of God. Hear Him! Hear Him when He says, "Come unto me all you that labour and are heavy laden and I will give your rest." Hear Him when He says, "I, if I am lifted up from the earth, will draw all men unto me." Hear Him, I say, hear Him. For "God was in Christ, reconciling the world unto Himself."

'But how! How shall we hear Him? He speaks in the word of Scripture. He speaks through His sent servants. He speaks by His Holy Spirit in the hearts of His people. Undoubtedly it becomes us to listen with devout reverence. Let us revere every sacred truth of Scripture.

'As a pupil in the school of Christ, will you violate His laws because you will only be put to the bottom of the class, and no one supposes you will be expelled from the school? Has it come to this with you, professing Christian, that to escape from Hell is the only thing you care about? Each member of the whole church should be jealous of every minute particle of the Truth of God.

'And let us hear believingly. And, as it is a custom to keep His word, let us always hear Him expectantly.

'So, lastly, when shall we hear him? The reply must be "For evermore!" Hear Him when you begin your Christian career. "Hear and your soul shall live" and "Faith comes by hearing, and hearing by the word of God".

'And do you not think, dear friends, it would be well that believers should have a special time for hearing Christ every day? Mark off a quarter of an hour each day for hearing what God the Lord should speak. We have the rush and the crash of the world in our ears nearly all day. If we want to hear Christ's voice, we must sometimes sit alone in silence. He will be poor who does not set apart some time in which he can listen to the voice of Christ by searching the Scriptures, by drawing near to God, by watching and prayer.

'"Hear you Him," my brothers and sisters. "Hear you Him." The Lord unstop your ears now, O you that have never heard Him, O you that have heard Him often, hear Him now. And hear Him more often until He shall say unto you, "Come up here," and you shall finally enter into His joy. God bless each one of us for Christ's sake. Amen.'

Throughout that great church there was silence as Spurgeon paused for a few moments to let the message sink in. He then announced the final hymn, the precentor set the tune and once more music filled the Tabernacle.

After he had uttered the benediction, the people gradually left the building. But in various parts of the Tabernacle little clusters of two or three people could be seen, as those who had heard Christ for many years counselled those who were just beginning to hear.

***

It would be a mistake to suppose that everything flowed smoothly at the Tabernacle. On occasions a member would fall into sin or would stop attending the services, and that had to be dealt with. The process adopted was that first elders or other appointed leaders were sent to interview the individual concerned to try to establish the truth of the situation. If the person had just stopped attending and had no intention of returning, then their names were removed from the roll.

In the instances of accusations of sin, if the visitors had good reason to believe that the charges were true, then that person was urged to repent. In regard to this, it was not enough for the individual to say they were sorry. It was necessary for them to declare that they would reform their behaviour. If a member was not repentant, then they were removed from the church roll. When someone was removed from the roll for disciplinary reasons, it was announced to the members but the details were not given. However, the church was always open to those individuals who mended their ways at a later date and sought to rejoin the church. The leaders of the Tabernacle always hoped for the restoration of those who had fallen away.

***

In 1867 it became necessary to make some structural alterations to the Tabernacle. During the five weeks while this took place, Spurgeon preached at the Agricultural Hall in Islington on the northern side of the river. That hall held 18,000 to 20,000 people, yet it was full each week. Further redecorating was carried out at the Tabernacle 16 years later and Spurgeon returned to the Exeter Hall for the last time.

CHAPTER 15

SPURGEON AS A WRITER

Spurgeon was an avid reader. He read much profound theology but his reading did not end there, for he seemed delighted to engage his mind in almost any topic. For much of his ministerial career, in spite of his busyness, he read about five books a week. This helped keep his preaching fresh. It also encouraged him to write. His sermons and lectures appeared in book form, but other books that bear his name were literally written. He also wrote hundreds of articles for *The Sword and the Trowel*.

Spurgeon didn't find it easy to write. Public speaking and writing are two different means of expression, and few succeed at both. He once wrote, 'Writing is to me the work of a slave. It is a delight to me to talk out my thoughts in words that flash upon the mind at the instant they are required, but it is poor drudgery to sit still and groan for thoughts and words without obtaining them.' But whatever the struggle, Spurgeon did write and he succeeded as a writer.

When Spurgeon was living in Stambourne during his childhood, he met a ploughman named William Richardson. The ploughman was not well educated but was able to read and write. He was also a godly man and well-versed in the Scriptures. He impressed the young boy with his homely wisdom and Spurgeon never forgot the lessons he learned from him. Sometimes when Will was ploughing, young Charles would walk beside him and take delight in listening to his quaint sayings.

Many years later Spurgeon wrote two little books: *John Ploughman's Talk* and *John Ploughman's Pictures*. While these were written with Spurgeon's own inimitable wit, many of the lessons they taught he had learnt from Will Richardson.

In July 1870 Will was dying and Spurgeon had the privilege of visiting him on his deathbed. Will was coherent and as faithful to Christ while dying as he had been behind the plough in the full strength of his manhood. Spurgeon began to read John chapter 17 to him, which contains that wonderful prayer of God the Son to God the Father.

As Spurgeon began Will shouted out, 'Oh, that is my blood horse!'

The preacher stopped, a little confused. 'What do you mean, Will?'

Richardson replied, 'I can ride higher on that chapter than on any other.'

Spurgeon smiled and continued with the reading.

Four days later, Will Richardson went to be with his Lord.

Some of the stories in the *John Ploughman* books will be familiar to many, though mainly because Charles Spurgeon made them so, directly or indirectly. The first of these books begins with a chapter called 'To the Idle'. One could not meet a man less idle than Spurgeon but he knew his subject well. 'It is of no more use to give advice to the idle than to pour water into a sieve; and as to improving them, one might as well try to fatten a greyhound.'

Then there was 'Things not worth trying'. One of these 'things' was 'It is a silly thing to preach to drunken men. It is casting pearls before swine. First get them sober, and then talk to them soberly.' Another was 'Many preachers are good tailors spoiled, and capital shoemakers turned out of their proper calling. When God wishes a creature to fly, He gives it wings, and when He intends men to preach He gives them abilities.' (While this principle is generally true, it may contradict Spurgeon's own conversion experience. According to Spurgeon, the preacher on that occasion had little ability, but Spurgeon still became a Christian through his stuttering and repetitious sermon.)

In addition, there was the famous story, 'He who would please all will lose his donkey.' While this was not original to Spurgeon, he told it with his own colourful embellishments. In this story a man and his son were walking with their donkey to market. A man saw them and ridiculed them for walking and not riding the animal. So the son mounted the beast. They then met another man who called the boy 'a lazy rogue' for riding the donkey while the father had to walk. So they changed places. The father rode, while the boy walked. Inevitably they met another man, who called the father a 'knave' for riding, while his son had 'to creep after him'. So the son joined his father on the donkey and they both rode the poor animal. The next passer-by accused them of being cruel to the donkey for over-loading it. The story ended with the man and his son carrying the donkey to the market where they were laughed at for their trouble.

Spurgeon's applications of this story were pithy and sensible. 'He who will not go to bed until he pleases everybody will have to stay up a good many nights', he wrote, and 'if we please one person we are sure to set another grumbling'. Those were wise words for his Victorian listeners, but even wiser words for us in our age, when it seems to be regarded as a criminal act to offend anyone. As Spurgeon said, 'What is there, after all, to frighten a man in a fool's grin, or in the frown of a poor mortal like yourself? A true man does what he thinks is right, whether the pigs grunt or the dogs howl.'

It is all practical wisdom. As one reads these brief chapters, one becomes aware of why Spurgeon appealed to so many people. He could grapple with profound truth but he did so in a way that even simple people could understand, and all in brilliant colour. It says much for his writing and preaching that even though he had a powerful intellect, he could still be understood by simple people. Not many can achieve that.

Amongst his other books are *Around the Wicket Gate*, which as its sub-title said, is *A Friendly Talk with Seekers Concerning Faith in the Lord Jesus Christ*, and *The Cheque Book on the Bank of Faith*, which is a selection of biblical promises with comments by Spurgeon, arranged for daily reading. Also, from the heart of his mission, was *The Soul-Winner: How to Lead Sinners to the Saviour*. Towards the end of his life he also wrote his two-volume autobiography, though this was not published until after his death and was clearly heavily edited. Perhaps most momentous was his multi-volume *Treasury of David*, which was a commentary on the Psalms that Spurgeon had pieced together over a number of years. He found great comfort in these ancient poems. In the *Treasury* he included the wisdom of many preachers of earlier periods, particularly his favourite puritans.

He also wrote many articles in *The Sword and the Trowel*. These covered a host of subjects, the titles of which often make clear their theme. There was 'Among the Quakers', in which he made more complimentary than critical comments about the Society of Friends. Then there was the more provocative 'Churchianity versus Christianity', in which he was critical of the Church of England, and 'Anticipating the Last Judgment', in which his views on the End were clear and challenging but not extreme.

One article that has great relevance for our own age is 'Advanced Thinkers', in which Spurgeon said,

'There has by degrees risen up in this country a coterie, more than ordinarily pretentious, whose favourite cant is made up of such terms as these: "liberal views", "men of high culture", "persons of enlarged minds and cultivated intellects", "bonds of dogmatism and the slavery of creeds", "modern thought" and so on. That these gentlemen are not so thoroughly educated as they fancy themselves to be, is clear from their incessant boasts of their culture; that they are not free, is shrewdly guessed from their loud brags of liberty; and that they are not liberal, but intolerant to the last degree, is evident.'

In this article he also uses a striking phrase, 'that bigotry for liberality'. This all rings true today too. We hear the same boasts and encounter the same blindness.

Spurgeon also wrote a number of hymns, some of which have long survived him. They include:

Sweetly the holy hymn
Breaks on the morning air;
Before the world with smoke is dim
We meet to offer prayer.

and

Amidst us our Beloved stands,
And bids us view his pierced hands;
Points to his wounded feet and side,
Blest emblems of the Crucified.

Spurgeon's books have sold many million copies. They have defeated the tyranny of time and even today thousands read his sermons, his lectures on preaching, his *Ploughman* books and his articles from *The Sword and the Trowel*. He is still one of the most widely read Christian authors.

CHAPTER 16

BAD DAYS; GOOD DAYS

Spurgeon once wrote:

'Before I came to London, I usually preached three times on the Lord's Day and five nights every week; and after I became Pastor at New Park Street Chapel, that average was fully maintained. Within two or three years, it was considerably exceeded, for it was no uncommon experience for me to preach twelve or thirteen times a week, and to travel hundreds of miles by road or rail. Requests to take services in all parts of the metropolis and the provinces poured in upon me, and being in the full vigour of early manhood, I gladly availed myself of every opportunity of preaching the gospel which had been so greatly blessed to my own soul. In after years, when weakness and pain prevented me from doing all that I would willingly have done for my dear Lord, I often comforted myself with the thought that I did serve Him with all my might while I could, though even then I always felt that I could never do enough for Him who had loved me, and given Himself for me.'

For much of his later life Charles Spurgeon lived with various degrees of suffering, some of it most severe, from a variety of medical conditions. He had gout, rheumatism, lumbago, nephritis (also known as Bright's Disease, a painful kidney condition), and in his final year a bad case of influenza, all topped off by frequent bouts of depression. He once said, 'I pity the dog that has felt as much pain in four legs as I have felt in one.' Sometimes the pain was so bad in his hands that he could not hold a pen to write. He regarded these conditions as from the chastening hand of his loving heavenly Father. But they were still hard to bear.

Though there were specific causes for these individual conditions, the one that seemed to drive them all was stress. Spurgeon's work load in his church and its associated ministries was colossal. While he had able lieutenants, such as his brother James and his secretary Joseph Harrald, many matters still required his attention. When funds were needed for, say, the orphanage, if one of his helpers sent out a letter asking for money, the results were moderate. If Spurgeon himself sent out the letter in his unmistakable style, the results were far greater. This assured more work for him.

In addition to his work at home, many other churches and Christian ministries wanted him to speak at their functions, which only added to his burdens, even when he said 'No!' Often he wished to accept a request, but on the occasions when he did, the extra work usually worsened his health.

The Downgrade Controversy towards the end of his life also caused him much pain, emotionally and physically. That even some friends opposed him on this matter hurt him greatly. He viewed the Baptist Church in Britain as being on the slippery downhill slide with regard to sound doctrine. This caused him much distress, which further aggravated his physical ailments.

It will seem strange to many that he regarded these afflictions as coming from his loving Father God, but he did. As far back as 1857, before the severe decline in his health, he said in a sermon,

'[God] casts the Christian down; he gives the most afflictions
to the most pious; perhaps he makes more waves of trouble roll

over the breast of the most sanctified Christian than over the heart of any other man living. So, then, we must remember that as this world is not the place of punishment, we are to expect punishment and reward in the world to come; and we must believe that the only reason, then, why God afflicts his people must be this:

"'In love I correct thee, thy gold to refine,
To make thee at length in my likeness to shine.'"

Twenty-nine years later, amidst great physical suffering, he said in one sermon on rejoicing:

'I believe that one of the sweetest joys under heaven comes out of the severest suffering when patience is brought into play. "Sweet," says Toplady, "to lie passive in thy hand, and know no will but thine." And it is so sweet, so inexpressibly sweet, that to my experience the joy that comes of perfect patience is, under certain aspects, the divinest of all the joys that Christians know this side of heaven. The abyss of agony has a pearl in it which is not to be found upon the mountain of delight. Put patience to her perfect work, and she will bring you the power to rejoice evermore.'

He suffered and while he was not pleased that he did, he was delighted that he seemed to catch a clearer vision of God amidst that suffering. The pain was hard to endure but it seemed to give him a greater experience of Christ, who had suffered for him.

Spurgeon frequently spent winter weeks in Menton (or Mentone) in south-eastern France near the Franco-Italian border where the weather was mild during the colder months and better for his health. In 1861 James Henry Bennet, a doctor, published a book entitled *Winter and Spring on the Shores of the Mediterranean*, which promoted this resort as an ideal spot for people in poor health. It became a popular destination for ailing Britons, and the number of its hotels increased from two or three to more than 30 in the 14 years after the book's publication. Queen Victoria, Lord Shaftesbury, George Müller, and the writers Robert Louis Stevenson and Katherine Mansfield were other famous visitors to Menton.

***

In 1884 Charles Spurgeon reached the age of 50. The leaders of his church decided that the event would be warmly celebrated. It would be a Jubilee. However, the year did not start well. In the winter, he paid his customary visit to Menton, but on this occasion his health did not recover, at least not as quickly as hoped. He had to delay his return to London because he was too unwell, and even when he did return he was too ill to preach on some Sundays.

After two weeks of being unable to preach, at the end of winter he wrote to his people, saying,

'Dear Friends,

It is to my intense sorrow that I find myself 'shut up' for another week. I hoped that I had escaped my enemy among the olives, but he threw me down at my own door. The Lord's will must be done, and we are bound to bear it without a repining thought. I shall not fall lower, but the difficulty is rising again. I am a poor creature. Evidently I am in the extreme of physical weakness. Nevertheless the Lord can cause his spiritual power to be shown in me, and I believe he will. Your great love will bear with me, and I shall be in the front again, bearing witness to the faithfulness of the Lord.'

He also worried that he was losing his power as a preacher. He found sermon preparation more difficult. This was partly due to his physical condition and partly due to the difficulty of producing something fresh for the ears of people who had heard him many times before. He had also noted over the years, that as some preachers aged, their sermons became longer, and he made a definite attempt to avoid this. He said, 'It would be a pity to shorten our congregation by lengthening our discourse.'

As to the Jubilee, Spurgeon said that 'the jubilation of our Jubilee does not call for any great blowing of trumpets, but rather for uplifting of hand and heart in prayer to God for further help'. But others were more than happy to blow the trumpets.

The Jubilee celebration began on Wednesday, 18 June 1884. On that day Spurgeon sat in the church vestry throughout the afternoon as many friends came to greet him and make contributions to the testimonial fund that had been set up in his honour. This was followed by a tea and a service in the Tabernacle. So many wanted to attend the service that a second had to be held, and even then there were not enough seats for all those wishing to attend.

It was a joyous occasion and a family occasion. Spurgeon's father, brother and son, Charles all spoke. But perhaps the most significant speaker that evening was D L Moody, the American evangelist, who was approaching the end of his second evangelistic tour of Britain. He said,

'Mr Spurgeon has said, tonight, that he has felt like weeping. I have tried to keep back the tears, but I have not succeeded very well. Twenty-five years ago, after I was converted, I began to read of a young man preaching in London with great power, and a desire seized me to hear him, never expecting that, some day, I should myself be a preacher. Everything I could get hold of in print that he ever said, I read. I knew very little about religious things when I was converted. I did not have what he has had: a praying father. My father died before I was four years old. I was thinking of that, tonight, as I saw Mr Spurgeon's venerable father here by his side.

'In 1867 I made my way across the sea. The first place to which I came was this building. I was told that I could not get in without a ticket, but I made up my mind to get in somehow, and I succeeded. I well remember seating myself in this gallery. I recollect the very seat, and I should like to take it back to America with me. As your dear Pastor walked down to the platform, my eyes just feasted upon him, and my heart's desire for years was at last accomplished.

'In 1872 I thought I would come over again to learn a little more, and I found my way back to this gallery. I have been here a great many times since, and I never come into the building without getting a blessing to my soul. I think I have had as great a one here tonight as at any other time I have been in this Tabernacle.

'But let me just say this, if God can use Mr Spurgeon, why should He not use the rest of us, and why should we not all just lay ourselves at the Master's feet, and say to Him, " Send me, use me?"'

But the joy of the event hid a dark cloud. The police had received word that a terrorist group was planning to blow up the Tabernacle during the Jubilee celebrations. There had been a number of such attacks at different locations the previous year and bombs had also been left at various railway stations in February of the year of the

Jubilee, though only one had exploded. At the end of May four more bombs were planted around London, including at police headquarters. Three of them exploded, resulting in ten injuries.

It was clear that the police had to take the threat seriously. A handful of Tabernacle officials were told about it, which led to an anxious time for them during the event, but the news was kept from Spurgeon until afterwards. Police, mainly in plain clothes, were scattered around the building and outside each evening, but the threat, if such it was, mercifully came to nothing.

CHAPTER 17

THE DOWNGRADE CONTROVERSY

When for the truth I suffer shame,
When foes pour scandal on Thy name,
When cruel taunts and jeers abound,
When 'bulls of Bashan' gird me round,
Secure within my tower I'll dwell,
That tower, Thy grace, Immanuel. (C H Spurgeon)

Though Spurgeon strongly believed in the Baptist Church as the most authentic form of church, he was not a bigot. He did at times criticise other denominations, but he could also heap praise on them, or at least individuals in those denominations. After all, he'd been brought up in two Congregational manses, been converted in a Primitive Methodist chapel and had plenty of opportunity to note the friendly relationship between his Congregational grandfather and the local Anglican rector. He also praised Wesleyan Methodism for sticking to the core teachings of the faith. He made clear what he believed and what he thought was wrong in the beliefs of others, but he still usually accepted as brothers and sisters those Christians who disagreed with him.

But then there was the Downgrade.

In 1859 Charles Darwin published his *On the Origin of Species*. This brought into doubt a literal interpretation of the early chapters of the Bible's first book, Genesis. Some Christians mocked Darwin's book, some ignored it, while others responded to it more positively. It made many ask questions about the reliability of the Bible.

Throughout the 19th century there had also emerged a movement that viewed the Bible as an ordinary book, with ordinary authors, which needed to be tested, examined and criticised like any other ordinary book. Those promoting these ideas did not generally regard the Bible as the word of God. This movement inevitably threw further doubt upon the reliability and divine origins of the Bible, which opened the way for the adoption of a host of questionable teachings and heresies.

This modernistic or liberal understanding of Scripture reached a crucial stage in Britain by the 1880s, in that it by then became common to teach it in many theological and ministerial training colleges.

These two distinct events coming so close together caused a shift in how many people understood the Bible. However, this took decades to develop and did not reach its peak until the early 20th century. Yet, it was evident to the astute observer in the 1880s, even before. Charles Haddon Spurgeon was an astute observer.

Spurgeon regarded these developments as the Downgrade.

The problem was made worse for the Baptist Union of England, to which Spurgeon and the Metropolitan Tabernacle belonged, in that it had no official statement of belief, no creed. Each cooperating church in that union was independent and it may or may not have had a statement of faith. There was no official statement about God, none about Christ, none about the Holy Spirit, none about the Bible and none about salvation. The Baptist Union's only requirement was that believers, and only believers, be baptised by immersion. But there was no official statement or guide as to what a person needed to believe to be a member of an English Baptist Church.

The Church of England had the *Thirty-nine Articles*, the Congregationalists and the Presbyterians had *The Westminster Confession* and the Methodists had *Wesley's Forty-Four Sermons* and *Wesley's Notes on the New Testament* to guide them. It's true that none of these statements of the faith were a sure protection against heresy (the Congregational Church did fall to modernism early), but they were statements of Christian belief to guide the churches and the faithful. The Baptist Union of England had nothing, or next to nothing.

Spurgeon had introduced an old Baptist adaption of *The Westminster Confession* for his own church late in 1855. And while he may have hoped other Baptist Churches would adopt it, there was no guarantee that any would.

When the strong winds of modernism swept in, by what standards were Baptist clergy and laity to judge the truth? One could answer, 'Judge it by the Bible.' But the Bible was under severe attack, and in the climate that was sweeping into England, one could accept which parts of the Bible one liked and reject those that one disliked.

Spurgeon saw the trend. He also saw the special danger that Baptist churches were in, for he knew these ideas were being adopted by some English Baptist scholars and younger pastors in the 1880s. News came to him from various quarters about certain individual Baptist clergy teaching ideas contrary to traditional Baptist beliefs. He only accepted these reports if they came from people he knew were reliable, but there were sufficient of these to disturb him.

This situation concerned him deeply, so he fought it. However, in his attack on the Downgrade, Spurgeon did not name names. He knew the names well enough, but Spurgeon had promised those who had supplied the information, at least his main source, that he would not reveal the names of the 'offenders' to anyone. Indeed, to reveal them might be to reveal the identities of those who were the sources of the information and Spurgeon did not want to do that. The Rev S H Booth, Secretary of the Baptist Union, had been that primary source, and he was reluctant to go public with his accusations, even though they proved to be true. Spurgeon honoured his commitment to Booth and attacked the movement instead, without naming individuals, but was accused of making false claims.

One way in which Spurgeon attacked was to try to get the Baptist Union to adopt a clear statement of faith. Who was a true Baptist and who was not a true Baptist? He thought if they adopted a specific set of beliefs, then they could assess who really belonged in the Baptist Church and who did not.

Spurgeon launched an avalanche of correspondence on the subject to various leaders in the Baptist Union to stir them to action. His position was strengthened in that he was not the only one disturbed about recent attitudes to the Bible, for others also viewed these trends with concern. The issue of adopting a confession was discussed at a meeting of the Baptist Union but Spurgeon's proposal to adopt a uniform creed was rejected.

This was devastating to Spurgeon. He knew a confession was no guarantee against liberal trends, but it was at least a clear guide to Baptist, indeed Christian, belief. It would set down what was acceptable and what was not acceptable. But the Union decided against it and to continue with its statement on baptism as its only official teaching.

But Spurgeon was Spurgeon. He would not lie down dead and he had plenty of arrows to shoot and bows to shoot them with. He also had support. In March 1887, he published an article in *The Sword and the Trowel* called 'The Down Grade', written by one of his ministerial associates, Robert Shindler. Another article by Shindler followed in April, with a third in June. Shindler later claimed that though he wrote these articles, Spurgeon gave him some assistance and later approved them, though he did not necessarily agree with everything Shindler said. Spurgeon had been ill and was convalescing in Menton early that year, which was presumably the reason he did not take up the pen himself at that time.

Simply put, the theme of these articles was that the church had been sliding down a slope since the end of the Puritan era and it was now 'going down-hill at breakneck speed'. This comment, inserted at the beginning of Shindler's first article, appears to have been written by Spurgeon. Shindler began the March article by tracing the history of the 'slide' from 1662, the date of the Act of Uniformity, which led to 2,000 clergy being ejected from the Church of England for remaining true to their traditional beliefs. He then gave a brief history of questionable teaching, even heresy, that emerged in the various English churches in the 17th and 18th centuries. In this paper Shindler used the term 'the down grade' (also 'the down-grade') frequently.

The second Downgrade article appeared that April. It began with a note, once more probably the work of Spurgeon, which said, 'Again we call special attention to this most important theme. The growing evil demands the attention of all who desire the prosperity of the church of God.' In this second article Shindler continued to trace this history of English deviations from the truth, and some Baptists were included in this account.

Shindler made some criticism of Arminianism in his articles, and by so doing, was likely to alienate Methodists and some others who were true to the core teachings of Scripture. However, Spurgeon made it clear in some notes in the April issue that what was being argued was not about the issue of predestination, but about something more basic. He wrote, 'Our warfare is with men who are giving up the atoning sacrifice, denying the inspiration of Holy Scripture, and casting slurs upon justification by faith. The present struggle is not a debate upon the question of Calvinism or Arminianism, but of the truth of God versus the inventions of men.'

A further article by Shindler appeared in *The Sword and Trowel* in June. This focused mainly on the Andover Seminary in America, which had begun as a thoroughly evangelical institution, but had now adopted a liberal understanding of the Bible and theology. Shindler warned that what had happened to Andover was happening in some theological colleges in Britain and could happen in others.

In August, Spurgeon, now in better health, entered more fully into the fray with an article called 'The Down Grade Controversy' or 'Another Word Concerning the Down Grade'.

'No lover of the gospel can conceal from himself the fact that the days are evil,' he began. He then launched into a series of stunning observations, in which he pulled no punches.

'Our solemn conviction is that things are much worse in many churches than they seem to be, and are rapidly trending downward. Read those newspapers which represent the Broad School of Dissent, and ask yourself, "How much farther could they go? What doctrine remains to be abandoned? What other truth is to be the object of contempt?" A new religion has been initiated, which is no more Christianity than chalk is cheese; and this religion, being destitute of moral honesty, palms itself off as the old faith with slight improvements, and on this plea usurps pulpits which were erected for gospel preaching. The Atonement is scouted, the inspiration of Scripture is derided, the Holy Spirit is degraded into an influence, the punishment of sin is turned into fiction, and the resurrection into a myth, and yet these enemies of our faith expect us to call them brethren, and maintain a confederacy with them!'

He then went on to criticise the decline in the spiritual life of many Christians, which manifested itself in a lack of prayer and a love of 'questionable amusements'. He continued,

'An eminent minister, who is well versed in the records of Nonconformity, remarked to us the other day that he feared history was about to repeat itself among Dissenters. In days gone by, they aimed at being thought respectable, judicious, moderate, and learned, and, in consequence, they abandoned the Puritanic teaching with which they started, and toned down their doctrines. The spiritual life which had been the impelling cause of their dissent declined almost to death's door, and the very existence of evangelical Nonconformity was threatened. Then came the outburst of living godliness under Whitefield and Wesley, and with it new life for Dissent, and increased influence in every direction.

'Alas! Many are returning to the poisoned cups, which drugged that declining generation. Too many ministers are toying with the deadly cobra of "another gospel", in the form of "modern thought". As a consequence, their congregations are thinning.'

He was clear. He was bold. He was faithful to the Gospel. Spurgeon never believed in hiding his beliefs or changing them unless he had good scriptural reasons. However, in nailing his colours so clearly to the mast, he was bound to receive much criticism. But the article did not end there. He continued,

'Where the gospel is fully and powerfully preached, with the Holy Ghost sent down from heaven, our churches not only hold their own, but win converts; but when that which constitutes their strength is gone—we mean when the gospel is concealed, and the life of prayer is slighted—the whole thing becomes a mere form and fiction. For this thing our heart is sore grieved.

'The case is mournful. Certain ministers are making infidels. Avowed atheists are not a tenth as dangerous as those preachers who scatter doubt and stab at faith. A plain man told us the other day that two ministers had derided him because he thought we should pray for rain. A gracious woman bemoaned in my presence that a precious promise in Isaiah which had comforted her had been declared by her minister to be uninspired. It is a common thing to hear workingmen excuse their wickedness by the statement that there is no hell, "the parson says so".

'Germany was made unbelieving by her preachers, and England is following in her track. Attendance at places of worship is declining, and reverence for holy things is vanishing; and we solemnly believe this to be largely attributable to the scepticism which has flashed from the pulpit and spread among the people. Possibly the men who uttered the doubt never intended it to go so far; but none the less they have done the ill, and cannot undo it. Their own observation ought to teach them better. Have these advanced thinkers filled their own chapels? Have they, after all, prospered through discarding the old methods? Possibly, in a few cases genius and tact have carried these gentry over the destructive results of their ministry; but in many cases their pretty new theology has scattered their congregations. The places which the gospel filled the new nonsense has emptied, and will keep empty.

'These gentlemen desire to be let alone. They want no noise raised. Of course thieves hate watch-dogs, and love darkness. It is time that somebody should spring his rattle, and call attention to the way in which God is being robbed of his glory, and man of his hope.

'It now becomes a serious question how far those who abide by the faith once delivered to the saints should fraternize with those who have turned aside to another gospel. Christian love has its claims, and divisions are to be shunned as grievous evils; but how far are we justified in being in confederacy with those who are departing from the truth? It is a difficult question to answer so as to keep the balance of the duties. For the present it behoves believers to be cautious, lest they lend their support and countenance to the betrayers of the Lord. It is one thing to overleap all boundaries of denominational restriction for the truth's sake: this we hope all godly men will do more and more. It is quite another policy which would urge us to subordinate the maintenance of truth to denominational prosperity and unity.

'We fear it is hopeless ever to form a society which can keep out men base enough to profess one thing and believe another; but it might be possible to make an informal alliance among all who hold the Christianity of their fathers. Little as they might be able to do, they could at least protest, and as far as possible free themselves of that complicity which will be involved in a conspiracy of silence. If for a while the evangelicals are doomed to go down, let them die fighting, and in the full assurance that their gospel will have a resurrection when the inventions of "modern thought" shall be burned up with fire unquenchable.'

Inevitably, these articles drew criticism as well as praise, so in September Spurgeon published 'Our Reply to Sundry Critics and Enquirers'. In it he reported that some of the responses he had received indicated the situation was even worse than he had thought. 'It seems,' he wrote, 'that instead of being guilty of exaggeration, we should have been justified in the production of a far more terrible picture.' He added, 'But no one has set himself to disprove our allegations.' In other words, it would appear that the changes in Christian belief and behaviour that Spurgeon had mentioned were true. It was just a case of whether the changes were right or not.

According to this article, some argued that Spurgeon's poor health had affected his judgement and suggested that he needed 'to take a long rest'. Spurgeon protested that he was well enough when he wrote the August article, and he objected to some of his opponents attacking his person, instead of his arguments. Others argued that he had written in haste, thus without sufficient thought, and that had led him into unjust criticism of his fellow Christians. But Spurgeon's approach was not rushed. It was well thought out. He had spent much time considering the problem and how best to respond to it.

He had, by this time, received support from another publication, *Word and Work*. The editor of that journal praised, 'His exposure of the dishonesty which, under the cover of orthodoxy, assails the very foundations of faith.' That editor continued, 'Under the plea of liberalism, unscriptural doctrines are allowed' to appear 'in sermons and periodicals, which, only a few years ago, would have been faithfully resisted unto the death'.

In his 'reply' Spurgeon continued, 'That ugly word "pessimist" has been hurled at our devoted head. We are denounced as "gloomy"' [Note that Spurgeon often used 'our' and 'we' to refer to himself]. 'Well, well! The day was when we were censured for being wickedly humorous, and many were the floggings we received for our unseemly jests. Now we are morose and bitter.'

But this was not a case of Spurgeon being pessimistic, as at least one Christian publication had said. Spurgeon was 'glad to admit that there is much of Christian zeal, self-sacrifice and holy perseverance in the world. Possibly there is more than ever.' But that did not destroy the argument that there was also a growing movement in the churches promoting false teaching that was seriously damaging the Church of

Christ. In fact, much of the negative response to Spurgeon's claims only proved they were true.

Amidst the furore, Spurgeon had not lost his humour. 'Our amiable critics,' he said, 'may possibly be pleased to know that they will not find us bathing in vinegar, nor covering our swollen foot with wormwood, nor even drinking quinine with our vegetables; but they will find us rejoicing in the Lord and buckling on our harness for the war with as firm a confidence as if all men were on our side.'

Another problem had to be considered amongst all this: can Christians who hold to traditional evangelical beliefs 'keep company with those who do not? There must come with decision for truth,' Spurgeon argued, 'a corresponding protest against error. Let those who will keep the narrow way keep it, and suffer for their choice; but to hope to follow the broad road at the same time is an absurdity.'

In this fight Spurgeon was uncompromising. He said, 'It is my highest ambition to be clear of the blood of all men. I have preached God's truth, so far as I know it, and I have not been ashamed of its peculiarities. I have cut myself clear of those who err from the faith, and even from those who associate with them.' They were strong words and words that would lose him friends, but he felt that he had to make a firm stand.

To many people Spurgeon had now lost his aura. To some, he had become a nuisance and a man out of touch with his times. He was seen as causing trouble in the church. There were those, as we have seen, who put his words down to his sickness but it had nothing to do with that. Rather, it had everything to do with core Christian beliefs that he believed were unchangeable, but which some were trying to change.

The general meeting of the Baptist Union that year did not discuss the issue officially. It was almost as if it did not exist or did not matter. The official reason for that was that no charges had been laid against specific individuals, so no action could be taken. In truth, they probably regarded it as too hot to handle and too divisive. But it was certainly a well-discussed topic around the meeting's meal tables.

On 28 October 1887, inevitably it seems, Spurgeon resigned from the Baptist Union. He felt he had no alternative. Immediately afterwards the leaders of the Metropolitan Tabernacle published a statement supporting their pastor, and the Tabernacle withdrew from the Union the following year. It then became an independent body.

Little good had come out of the struggle, yet that was not Spurgeon's fault but rather his detractors. However, one positive aspect seems to have been that it caused some, who may have adopted modernist theology, to instead follow Spurgeon's example. His courage and faithfulness encouraged others.

This campaign was not a matter of Spurgeon being anti-scholarship or anti-intellectual. He had benefitted from some of the best scholarship of past eras and his own, and he was more than able to engage with the intelligent people of his time on a number of subjects. One book he published was *Commenting and Commentaries*, which examined biblical commentators and commentaries past and present. This book showed the vast extent of his reading but also his ability to assess scholarship intelligently. It was also clear from it that he was not negative about the science of Textual Criticism of the New Testament, that is, the establishing of the original Greek New Testament text, which was going on in his own lifetime. He also felt free to use the recently translated Revised Version of the Bible, and believed that in some places it shed new light upon the text.

However, the struggles of this campaign had caused a further decline in Spurgeon's health. The dreadful conflict weakened him considerably. It is also extraordinarily sad that the man who had done so much to promote the cause of the Baptist Union had to finish his ministry outside it.

CHAPTER 18

HIS FINAL DAYS

When down the hill of life I go,
When o'er my feet death's waters flow,
When in the deep'ning flood I sink,
When friends stand weeping on the brink,
I'll mingle with my last farewell
Thy lovely name, Immanuel. (C H Spurgeon)

It is unclear how Spurgeon became aware of Menton but it was probably from a member of his congregation or a ministerial colleague who had read Dr James Bennet's book about the health benefits of the area. As has been seen, when the winter months became too much for him, Spurgeon moved to Menton, usually leaving Susannah behind. Though these visits were great opportunities to rest, he frequently preached to what seemed to be an increasing congregation. While there, he also benefitted from Dr Bennet's medical skill.

When pain allowed, he also wrote letters and books. When the pain was too great, he dictated them. After one bad attack of gout he said, 'I feel as if I am emerging from a volcano,' so acute was the pain.

He left for his second last trip to Menton on 11 November 1890, accompanied by his secretary, Joseph Harrald. Susie, who was never in the best of health either, stayed at home. He did not return until 5 February the following year. He arrived at Menton in good spirits and the weather was warm, with 'heavenly sunshine' that made it seem 'like another world'. But the following day he was afflicted by severe gout in his right arm and hand, and the attack continued for more than a week.

Harrald reported that at times, Spurgeon was so distressed that he kept saying, 'I wish I were home' and 'I must get home.' But he was in no fit state to travel and Menton was better for him in winter, so he stayed. It was well he did for England had early snow at the end of November; the beginning of a harsh winter.

When the worst of the attack of gout had past, he wrote a letter in spidery handwriting to Susie with his left hand, saying, 'I am better except at night,' though 'better' does not seem to have meant he was well. He assured her of his love and praised God amidst all the suffering.

He wrote to her again on the first day of December, reporting that Menton had been hit by two fierce storms. 'The tempest howled, yelled, screamed and shrieked,' he told her. 'The heavens seemed on fire, and the skies reverberated like the boom of gigantic kettledrums.' A couple of days later he was able to get out in a carriage and reported that the day was 'so fair, so calm, so bright, so warm', in great contrast to the storms. The storms had done considerable damage and he encountered a number of villagers trying to clear the roads and carry out repairs. He and Harrald 'commiserated' with them.

As his health improved, he was able to lead morning worship for the English residents of the resort. He also visited an ageing Baroness and prayed with her. But he was soon unwell again. Once more, he made a partial recovery. He was able to spend Christmas Day 'digging away at books and letters' but at night 'his bones cried and groaned'.

On the first day of the New Year he was able to lead worship for the Menton community. He preached from Psalm 103, which begins 'Bless the Lord, O my soul; and all that is within me bless his holy name.' Later that day he was able to go for a drive in 'the delicious summer sunshine', even though it was mid-winter.

One Sunday he went to 'a Presbyterian place of worship', which, in fact, was a woman's garden. The preacher, J E Somerville, spoke on Rev. 2:12-17, the 'letter' to the angel at Pergamum, 'splendidly witnessing against the "Down-grade"'.

As January progressed, he recovered sufficiently to be able to do plenty of writing. He was also able to preach on occasions. At the beginning of February he reported to Susie 'I am very much better, indeed well,' and plans were made for his return to England. He left Menton on 5 February.

Soon after his return he began preaching again at the Tabernacle. He was also able to meet with prospective members and 84 of them were soon added to the church. In fact, it was reported at a business meeting in February 1891 that the membership of the Tabernacle was 5,328. In addition, it had 23 missions with a total seating capacity of over 3,500, and 27 Sunday Schools that had nearly 600 teachers and over 8,000 students. When one adds to this the other churches and ministries that had been founded or assisted by Spurgeon and his people and his writing ministry, one can see that the scope of the work was widespread and effective.

Towards the end of April he presided at the conference of the Pastors' College. This conference was a time of 'exhausting delight' for him and 'everything went well'.

But though his physical ailments had improved in the later stages of winter and early spring, they soon worsened again. One Sunday towards the end of April he 'entered the pulpit' to take the evening service, 'and was obliged to hurry out of it', he was so unwell. Fortunately William Stott, who had been employed recently as assistant pastor, was able to take over.

The following Sunday he was able to preach at both services

and for the remainder of that week, he was very busy. He counselled enquirers on Monday afternoon and presided at a prayer meeting that evening. He preached at Bloomsbury Chapel on Tuesday evening, at the Tabernacle on Thursday and spoke twice at a ministers' fraternal on Friday. To these meetings that week were added other duties, such as keeping up with his correspondence and other writing. It was enough work for a young man in good health, but Spurgeon was no longer young and his health, though improved, was not good.

On Sunday morning 17 May, he preached from 'My times are in thy hand' (Psalm 31:15), which, as things turned out, was a most appropriate message. There had been a virulent strain of influenza that year that had killed many. Now the flu caught up with him. It was a savage encounter and he was unable to preach that evening and on the two Sundays that followed.

By 7 June, he was sufficiently recovered to preach again at the Tabernacle. The passage on this occasion was 1 Samuel 30:21-25, which was about David and his favourable treatment of those unable to fight beside him. But the sermon inevitably shifted to Christ, who Spurgeon called, 'the most magnanimous of captains'. For, he continued, 'there never was his like among the choicest of princes'. In fact, this Christ 'is always to be found in the thickest part of the battle. The heaviest end of the cross lies ever on His shoulders. If He bids us carry a burden, He carries it also. If there is anything that is gracious, generous, kind and tender, yea lavish and superabundant in love, you always find it in Him. His service is life peace, joy. Oh, that you would enter on it at once! God help you to enlist under the banner of Jesus Christ.'

This proved to be his last sermon at the Tabernacle. He was, to the end, an evangelist.

A great concert of prayer burst forth for his recovery. It was not just Baptists who prayed for him, it was also the members of other non-conformist churches. It was not just the non-conformists who prayed for him but also people from the Church of England, including some leading dignitaries. Perhaps oddly, it was not just Christians who prayed for him, but even the Chief Rabbi of the Jewish community led his people on behalf of the great preacher, who had so boldly proclaimed Jesus as the Christ.

By the end of October, Spurgeon was well enough to travel, so he, Susannah, his brother, his brother's wife and Joseph Harrald left London for Menton. They arrived on 29 October.

At times during the following three months he was strong enough to continue writing for *The Sword and the Trowel,* and to do other editorial work on some of his books. Even on a couple of occasions in mid-January he was able to preach but these sermons were shorter than his usual efforts and bore the marks of his infirmity. The 'congregations' were also much smaller, containing as they did the small group that had travelled with him and a few other visitors to Menton.

As January progressed, his health declined further. One of his final acts was to send a donation of £100 for the Tabernacle from him and his beloved Susie.

In the last hour of January 1892 Charles Haddon Spurgeon went to be with his Lord, whom he had loved so much and served so faithfully and so successfully. Now he could see that Lord 'face to face'. As he had once written,

> When tears are banished from mine eyes,
> When fairer worlds than these are nigh,
> When heaven shall fill my ravished sight,
> When I shall bathe in sweet delight,
> One joy all joys shall far excel,

To see Thy face, Immanuel. (C H Spurgeon)

Susie was distressed but not destroyed. She later wrote, 'Ah! My husband, the blessed earthly ties which we welcomed so rapturously are dissolved now, and death has hidden thee from my mortal eyes; but not even death can divide thee from me, or sever the love which united our hearts so closely. I feel it living and growing still, and I believe it will find its full and spiritual development only when we shall meet in the glory-land, and worship "together before the throne".'

Prior to Spurgeon's body being sent back to England, a memorial service was held in the Scotch Presbyterian Church in Menton where Spurgeon had preached the previous year. His body was taken back to London on 8 February and initially placed in the common room of the Pastors' College. It was a foul and wet day, which matched the mood of the mourners. Later it was transported to the Tabernacle to await the funeral service.

More than 20 years before, a Nathaniel Plainspeech had condemned the extravagance of many funerals. 'What can possess some people to spend so much money on putting a poor corpse into the ground?' he asked. 'A plain coffin is all the dead can need, and enough help to bear the body to its last bed is all that is required.' It was better, he thought, to spend money on the living rather than the dead. As it happened, Nathaniel Plainspeech was a pseudonym for Charles Haddon Spurgeon. An elaborate funeral was not, then, according to the wishes of the deceased. In keeping with Spurgeon's views, it was requested that mourners make donations to the various Spurgeon charities rather than send flowers.

But inevitably the funeral and associated services would have to be a large affair, with so many wishing to pay their respects. In the end, services were held at the Tabernacle over a period of five days, and it was estimated that the total attendance was about 100,000. After these services he was buried in a cemetery in Norwood in the south of London, near where he had lived in his later years. Once more thousands gathered and shed tears as they said goodbye to 'The Prince of Preachers'.

***

Tributes came from near and far. They came from Baptists and non-Baptists, Christians and non-Christians. Amongst his fellow-labourers at the Tabernacle, T H Olney, a deacon, said, 'I must bear testimony that he inspired very great confidence in us all. We, as deacons, had very little to do but back him up.' William Olney, another deacon, said, 'Our dear pastor had a remarkable power of infusing his own love for souls into the hearts of others.' Elder J T Dunn remembered, 'When persons came to enquire concerning salvation, or to confess their faith in the Lord Jesus Christ, how his eyes would brighten, and how heartily he would welcome them.'

Joseph Parker, a Congregational preacher who had crossed swords with Spurgeon over the Downgrade Controversy, said that he had 'the mightiest voice I ever heard' and that his preaching 'proved that evangelical teaching can draw around itself the greatest congregation in the world, and hold it for a lifetime'.

Arthur T Pierson, an American Presbyterian, called him 'a genius in the intellectual sphere', 'a genius in the moral sphere' and 'a genius in the spiritual sphere'. He added that Spurgeon 'spoke in tones convincing and persuasive' and 'gave new strength and encouragement to many a stricken one'.

The Archdeacon of St Paul's Cathedral called him Britain's 'greatest living preacher', even though he was no longer living. The Archdeacon continued, 'He had that genuine eloquence which is all the more effective because of its directness and simplicity. He had a matchless voice, powerful and vibrating with every quality of earnestness and variety. He had abundant humour, tender pathos, and never failed to be interesting. But it was above all the exuberant vitality of his faith in God's revelation through His Son Jesus Christ, combined with the width and warmth of his zealous love for souls that gave him that unbounded power.'

CHAPTER 19

'THE ECHO OF HIS VOICE'

'While time shall last, the echo of his voice will be heard' (*The Episcopal Recorder,* 17 March 1892).

God alone knows how many were converted through Spurgeon's ministry, as it is impossible to keep such records. But in an *In Memorium* issued by the Tabernacle after his death it was stated that 14,691 had been added to that church's 'communion-roll during his pastorate'. Whilst hundreds of those would have come from other churches and were converted through other ministries, it is probable that most of that number would have been converted under Spurgeon's ministry.

In addition, many were converted at New Park Street and the Metropolitan Tabernacle, who linked with other churches. And to that can be added those who were converted through Spurgeon's preaching during his visits to other areas and through his writing. Even today his works are read and they still bear fruit.

Charles Haddon Spurgeon had established an astonishing work at the Metropolitan Tabernacle. The questions now were: *would it collapse after his passing or would it go from strength to strength? And who would replace him?* There would certainly not be another like him, for he was unique.

Spurgeon had speculated some time before, 'Who knows where my successor may be? He may be in America, or in Australia, or I know not where. As for the Tabernacle, the man who occupies my place, when I pass away, will have to depend upon his own resources, upon the support of his people, and the grace of God, as I have done; and if he cannot do that, let him come to the ground, for he will not be the fitting man for the post.'

His immediate successor was, in fact, an American, Arthur T Pierson. Oddly, bearing in mind that the Tabernacle was a Baptist Church, he was a Presbyterian. Pierson had preached at the Tabernacle on a number of occasions from 1889 and stood in for Spurgeon during his final illness. Though he, like Spurgeon, rejected the Downgrade, his theology, which was dispensational, was different from his predecessor.

Inevitably, Pierson's term as pastor at the Tabernacle did not last long. His replacement was an Englishman who had spent a number of years serving in Australia and New Zealand. This was none other than Thomas Spurgeon, son of Charles and Susie. It must be difficult for the sons of outstanding men. If they follow the same or similar careers to their fathers they will always be compared with them and it is hard to match the great. Thomas Spurgeon was a good, successful preacher in his own right and a godly man, but he did not have the ability of his father.

Under his ministry the Tabernacle still attracted good attendances and its various ministries continued on satisfactorily but the fire had gone. In 1898 a fire of a different kind destroyed the building. The church met in temporary accommodation for about three years while the Tabernacle was rebuilt. But the leaders were realistic and it was a smaller building than its predecessor. Thomas Spurgeon resigned on the grounds of ill health in 1907.

Several other pastors followed and the second building suffered severe bomb damage during the Second World War. Once again, it was successfully repaired and the church continued its ministry, though with much smaller congregations. It also rejoined the Baptist Union.

By 1970 the congregation had become tiny. But since then it has undergone a transformation under the leadership of Peter Masters. Today its services are well attended, with simultaneous translations in Korean, Spanish, Chinese and French. It also has a ministry to people who are deaf. Amongst its other many ministries are a Sunday School that teaches the gospel to hundreds of south London children, and a Reformed Baptist Seminary. In addition, *The Sword and the Trowel* continues on. Peter Masters, like Spurgeon, opposes the Downgrade, and under his leadership the Metropolitan Tabernacle has again become an independent Baptist Church.

But Spurgeon's influence has spread much further than the Metropolitan Tabernacle. As has been seen, Spurgeon's ministry led to the establishing and growth of numerous Baptist churches in England. While some of these have now closed, others have continued on.

In his lifetime Spurgeon had influence overseas through his writings, through missionaries sent out by the Tabernacle, and even through the ministry of his son Thomas in Australia and New Zealand. In fact, the majority of Baptist pastors who went from England to Australia in the last third of the 19th century had been trained at Spurgeon's Pastors' College and they had an ongoing influence there.

Though Spurgeon never travelled any further than Europe, his writings have travelled the world. His books and articles were read widely during his lifetime and they are still read widely today. A remarkable example of this is Pilgrim Publications, which is a company in Pasadena, Texas, which publishes a vast array of books by Spurgeon, including all his sermons but few books by other authors. Pilgrim's New Park Street and Metropolitan Tabernacle Pulpit series alone has 63 volumes. These and other books by Spurgeon are widely distributed and widely read.

In these ways and others, Charles Haddon Spurgeon's voice is still heard.

Also available from David Malcolm Bennett

John Wesley: *The man, his mission and his message.*

ISBN: 978-1-925139-27-3
$16.99 paperback
Release date: 1st June 2015

John Wesley, the founder of Methodism, was a great evangelist. He toured the British Isles for fifty years in the eighteenth century, preaching in churches, tiny chapels, village squares and in vast open areas, where he attracted enormous crowds. By the 1770s he was probably the most recognisable man in Britain, so much did he travel.

He was also a sensitive counsellor, a concerned pastor, a thoughtful theologian and a brilliant organiser. There are some who believe that his influence was so great that he and his associates saved England from the ravages of a revolution similar to that which occurred in France at the end of that century.

John Wesley: The Man, his Mission and his Message paints a picture of Wesley that is vivid and enduring. He appears in these pages as a real man, not a plastic saint, with all his astonishing talents, his clever sense of humour and his tragic weaknesses.

From Ashes to Glory

ISBN: 978-1-921632-76-1
$18.99 paperback
Release date: 1 March 2014
Joint Winner of the 2014 CALEB Award: Biography category

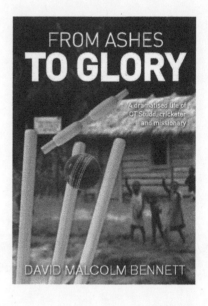

A Dramaticised retelling of CT Studd, his cricket, his mission work and the decisions he made which helped form the mission organisation WEC International.

CT (Charlie) Studd was a cricketer of the highest class. He played in the famed Test Match between England and Australia in 1882 that began the legend of the Ashes. From Ashes to Glory tells the story of this remarkable, dedicated man, and contains an authentic account of the 1882 Ashes Test, with all its drama.

At the peak of his fame Studd retired from cricket to serve as a missionary in China. In 1885 he was one of seven men of wealth and privilege ('The Cambridge Seven'), who shocked the nation, by giving up everything to take the Gospel of Jesus Christ to the Chinese. While there he suffered much, but saw many people come to Christ. He later spent six years as a missionary in India, where he opened a school which is still serving the community today.